30 Life Lessons My Boys Learned from Baseball

Especially for
K. Rob

Especially for
K. Rob

30 Life Lessons My Boys Learned from Baseball

Andy Norwood

PELICAN PUBLISHING COMPANY
GRETNA 2010

Copyright © 2008
By Andy Norwood
All rights reserved

Privately printed, 2008
First Pelican edition, 2010

The word "Pelican" and the depiction of a pelican
are trademarks of Pelican Publishing Company, Inc.,
and are registered in the U.S. Patent and Trademark Office.

Library of Congress Cataloging-in-Publication Data

Norwood, Andy.
   30 life lessons my boys learned from baseball / Andy Norwood. — 1st pelican ed.
     p. cm.
   ISBN 978-1-58980-794-5 (hardcover : alk. paper) 1. Baseball. 2. Baseball for children. 3. Father and child. 4. Character. I. Title. II. Title: Thirty life lessons my boys learned from baseball.
   GV867.N67 2010
   796.357—dc22
                           2010006033

Printed in the United States of America
Published by Pelican Publishing Company, Inc.
1000 Burmaster Street, Gretna, Louisiana 70053

*To my sons, Rob and Patrick, with appreciation
for the joy their play has brought to my life;
to my wife, Shannon, their biggest fan, who cheered them on,
treated their scrapes, dried their tears, and put up with
endless hours of infield and batting practice;
and to all the boys and girls who play baseball and
the adults who love, help, and encourage them*

Contents

	Introduction	9
Lesson #30	Don't Take Anything for Granted	15
Lesson #29	No Whining	21
Lesson #28	Some Days You're the Bat, Some Days You're the Ball	24
Lesson #27	Respect for Authority	28
Lesson #26	How to Deal with Different Kinds of People	34
Lesson #25	Control Your Emotions	38
Lesson #24	Math Counts	44
Lesson #23	Bridging the Generation Gap	47
Lesson #22	Competing with Your Friends	50
Lesson #21	Work Within Your Own Personality	53
Lesson #20	Perform under Pressure	58
Lesson #19	You Can Learn Almost Anything	62
Lesson #18	Toughness	65
Lesson #17	100 Percent or Concentrate	68
Lesson #16	Don't Waste Your Time on Something You Hate	72
Lesson #15	You Can't Do Anything about the Rain	78
Lesson #14	Courage	81
Lesson #13	Be Ready	85
Lesson #12	Take Advantage of Your Opportunities	91
Lesson #11	Everyone Can Contribute	97
Lesson #10	Practice Does Not Make Perfect, But . . .	101
Lesson #9	There's No Substitute for God-Given Ability	103
Lesson #8	Winning Is Important	107
Lesson #7	Don't Give Up	110
Lesson #6	Some Rules Have Reasons	114

Lesson #5	Play Fair	116
Lesson #4	Working on a Team	117
Lesson #3	How to Lose	124
Lesson #2	How to Win	129
Lesson #1	We Love You	133

Introduction

Both of my sons are big baseball fans. It's my fault. It's also something of which I am extremely proud.

I could give you a lot of folderol about the metaphysical components of the game, its elegant geometry, how there's something elemental in boys that draws them to this most beautiful and precise of all the sports—I believe all that, but it would not be the reason I made them fans. The truth is, they were weaned on it. Literally.

As first-time parents, we read all the books, talked to the grandparents, and worried ourselves sick about the everyday problems of raising a baby. One particularly challenging issue was how to get the baby to give up his last bottle of the day.

My older son, Rob, didn't think giving up his bottle was a big deal—except for that last bottle of the day. To be honest, this was partly my fault. When I was in town, giving Rob a last bottle and putting him down in his crib was my job. Mom usually headed for bed or a well-deserved break, and I would take over duties at the tail end of the day. Rob and I would sit together and I'd give him his last bottle of the day.

In time, that was the only bottle he took, drinking from a cup the rest of the day. In the spring, when even I had to admit that this special time for me and my son was ending forever (the first of many such endings, I sentimentally and correctly supposed), we started watching baseball on television.

Truthfully, I started watching baseball and describing it to Rob as if he was thirteen years old, not thirteen months. I fed him baseball instead of a bottle. This became our nightly ritual. Mom even started to stay up to watch a few innings with us. Eventually, around the bottom of the fifth, Rob would go to sleep, house finally quiet and all settled down for the night. By the All-Star break, neither of us really remembered that he used to take a bottle.

When Patrick came along, we were a lot more relaxed about things, as are most parents. Someone, I think Erma Bombeck, said about second children, "You find out the baby can kiss the dog and not die." Part of the relaxation is that you know you did it successfully once, and odds are you can do it again.

All kids are different—some days, ours don't even seem like brothers—but learning the basic stuff was pretty much the same for both. Patrick was content to sit with Rob and me, ignore his bottle, and listen in as I explained the game, play by play. By the age of three, Rob was ready to do a little play by play himself.

When Patrick was almost three, Rob was ready for the local Tee Ball league. Watching him out there on the diamond as he strived to copy what he had seen on television all those nights, I realized that he was moving out into the world on his own. While he was out there, he needed to learn some rules to help him survive. It wasn't only the rules of baseball I wanted Rob (and later Patrick) to learn out there on the field. I felt it was my obligation to teach my sons the lessons of life, and I saw the baseball diamond as the perfect classroom for that education. Corny, but true.

By "lessons" I don't mean the basic ones in those how-to books about kindergarten (share, flush) and I don't mean the more complex ones that they'll have to learn for themselves ("I have to stay home and wash my hair" really means "I'd rather kiss a pine-tar rag than go on a date with you"). What I mean by lessons are the concepts that help you get by and make you a little bit more successful in the world, or at least more successful than those who do not understand the subtle complexities of baseball.

I can't remember exactly how my father taught me these lessons, but I know he did. The parenting books were no help to me, and I was too embarrassed to keep questioning the grandparents. At some point I decided that I would try to use baseball to teach my sons the lessons that apply on either side of the white lines. Some of these lessons are not particularly friendly; in fact, many are harsh. I'll be the first one to say that my list isn't perfect—it is not even intended to be comprehensive.

You might make a good case that basketball, soccer, or synchronized team swimming may have just as much or more to recommend them for lessons on life. Sunday school and nightly reading from *The Book of Virtues* are certainly more appropriate for some areas. But baseball was something I understood and something the boys wanted to do, and trying this was better than admitting I had lost my copy of *How to Raise a Happy, Healthy Child* that they give you at the hospital right after your first child is born. As my wife says, "Look, kid, you didn't come with an owner's manual—we are doing the best we can."

I found out that most of what I wanted my sons to learn from baseball wasn't about baseball. If you accidentally picked up this book thinking it was an instruction manual on fielding line drives, throwing fastballs, or hitting to the opposite field, I'm sorry. There's nothing like that in here and I'm not qualified to teach it.

If you want to find out why I encouraged my boys to play ball and what I wanted them to get out of it, read on.

Both my boys now know how to hit a curve ball and turn a double play. These are no small talents. But, because of baseball, each will take much more with him when he heads off alone into the big wide world.

30 Life Lessons My Boys Learned from Baseball

Lesson #30
Don't Take Anything for Granted

A man's accomplishments in life are the cumulative effect of his attention to detail.

—John Foster Dulles

Baseball requires attention to detail. If you take some things—no, if you take almost anything—for granted, the play or game may not turn out the way you planned and hoped.

You have to watch the ball from the time it leaves the bat till you see it in the web of your glove before you can begin to throw it. Coaches yell, "I need to see the button on the top of your cap." The point is, of course, that your head and eyes need to be focused down, down on the baseball as it rolls into your glove. Even in major league games you will occasionally see a professional baseball player forget this and let a ball roll under his glove, between his legs, and into the outfield.

This sort of attention to detail also means that you will be prepared if something strange happens at the last minute. Ask Fred Lindstrom and Bill Buckner.

During the 2006 major league season, the Atlanta Braves had a promising first baseman named Adam LaRoche. LaRoche was a good player with a very relaxed and natural swing. He was playing first base, a position where the Braves did not have an established, veteran player. LaRoche had hit well that season, including a three-run shot against the Dodgers in his first at bat of the season.

In fact, he ended the season with almost 100 RBIs. But there had been a bad play that stood out over all his accomplishments.

In a game against the Washington Nationals in mid-May, the Braves were clinging to a one-run lead. With two outs and no one on in the bottom of the fifth, LaRoche fielded a slow roller to first. He took it for granted that the hitter would jog slowly down the line on the obvious out.

So after fielding the ball, it first looked as though LaRoche would tag the runner coming down the line. Then he turned and slowly headed over to first for the out at the bag. A funny thing happened, though. The hitter, Nick Johnson, tore down the line like young Rickey Henderson. It was a close play, but the umpire called Johnson safe. The inning extended. Not only did Johnson eventually score, the Nationals scored three more runs before the Braves managed to get the last out in the fifth. The Braves lost that day.

Braves manager Bobby Cox was not a happy man. (In fact, it turned out that LaRoche had attention-deficit disorder and he began taking medicine to help control it.)

One season when my son played in the machine pitch league, we had a good player on our team that we will call Bobby Smith. Over the season we noticed something strange about Bobby. He played great at the weekday games but was terrible on Saturdays. Because we played every Saturday, this was a problem. The coaches could not figure it out. Perhaps Bobby stayed up too late on Friday night. Perhaps he just didn't like giving up Saturdays to play baseball. But the questions we asked did not get the answers we expected.

Things came to a head after Bobby had played great at shortstop on a Thursday night but on Saturday let a ball roll past him in the outfield and then turned away from the plate at bat *after the umpire had put a ball in the pitching machine.* Somebody had to talk to his parents, and as the scorekeeper and occasional third-base coach, I drew the short straw.

I called his mother and came straight to the point. You are probably way ahead of me on this one. It turned out that Bobby was ADD, and Mrs. Smith gave him his medicine on school days but not on the weekends. I stopped short of my first instinct, which was to yell into the phone, *"What in the name of Kennesaw Mountain Landis are you thinking?"* Instead, I just told her that Bobby could be a very good player, but I was concerned he was going to get hurt if he kept turning his back on the ball because he was not able to pay attention. I asked if for the few Saturdays we had remaining if she could give him his medication.

To her credit, Mrs. Smith was very nice and understanding. She started giving his medicine on Saturday mornings and Bobby made the All-Star team. I hope his mom gave him his medication before the All-Star game.

In baseball, as in life, ADD or not, you have to do what it takes to pay attention to the details.

Lots of people have said it—I think George Brett is the one I heard it from—"If you do a thousand little things right, the big things seem to take care of themselves." Baseball is a good way to learn this. Making a sacrifice bunt looks like the simplest thing in the world when you watch someone else do it correctly. It's a critical play to get a player into scoring position or even occasionally home from third.

Bunting, though, is harder than it looks. That is why you will almost always see even major league players congratulating a teammate who has successfully put down a sacrifice bunt. To do it right, you must hold the bat correctly, position yourself correctly in the batter's box, bend your knees, focus on the ball, accept the ball with the bat at the right height and angle to put it where you want it on the diamond, and be ready to run to put the necessary pressure on the defense. Where the bat hits the ball is crucial. Putting the ball in the air can be a disaster.

The batter must remember the game situation. If the pitch would not be a strike, it might be appropriate to pull back from the bunt.

One final thing: some pitchers tend to take it personally if a hitter tries to sacrifice, so the batter has to be alert in case the pitch is coming at his head. Taking care of all of these little things will make the sacrifice—the big thing—successful. Failing at any one of them can cost more than the bunt would gain.

Attention to detail is also necessary for other things you do in life, both the useful and the critical. For example, it is very valuable for cooking. Use the right ingredients, cook at the right temperatures, and keep careful track of the time, and you'll get much better results.

More critically, attention to detail counts in driving. Buckle your seatbelt, watch your speed, and signal and check your blind spot before changing lanes. Baseball is not the only place to learn that attention to detail is critical. Baseball may not even be the best place to learn that attention to detail is critical. However, baseball is a good place to learn this lesson and learn it well.

The second component of not taking anything for granted involves attention to detail too, but for a different reason. You shouldn't take anything for granted because nothing in this life is certain. Pay attention to and enjoy every detail of every day, especially the lucky days when you get to play baseball, because it'll be over before you know it.

This is one of life's hardest lessons to learn. When you are young, the time between Thanksgiving and Christmas seems like years. A lifetime seems endless. Life, though, like your chances to play baseball, is not endless. Most kids just finally reach a day when the time and effort required to play baseball outweigh the joy and excitement, and without looking back (at least right then) they hang up their spikes.

For others, their league has progressed beyond their skill and it's almost a relief to look at other pursuits. An unhappy child is one who still enjoys baseball but has no other level to move on to. The local recreation league maybe lacks fields, coaches, or even just players his age who still want to play, and the school team is not an option.

The most painful class of kids, literally and figuratively, are the kids who still want to play and have a place to play, but their bodies won't let them—bad knees, repaired shoulders, whatever reason. We had one teammate who loved to play baseball but a failing liver cost him his chance between the white lines at an age when going back was a very difficult thing to do.

The point is not that you should play baseball as long as you can, though I believe you should. The point is that whenever you reach that time where you cannot or do not want to play any longer, be sure you have paid enough attention to detail that you will have a good stock of memories.

Of course, these memories don't have to be all game-winning hits, diving stabs at line drives, or championship celebrations on the mound. Some of those memories will just be the joy of being on a team, the impossible green of the grass under your cleats, the unending blue of the sky over your cap, and the indescribable feel when the sweet spot on the bat meets the dead center of the white part of a fastball and the contact is so perfect that it is almost as if the ball did not hit the bat.

It can be the whistle of wind through the ear holes of a batting helmet as you swipe second on a pitcher who plunked you on that same helmet and put you on first. It may just be a coach who called you at home after a game-winning hit to tell you he was so excited after the game he forgot to shake your hand, but it was "a great hit you got, son, just great."

Do not take any of those details for granted because—trust ol' Dad on this one—however it happens, they'll be gone all too soon.

Lesson #29
No Whining

Whining is not only graceless, but can be dangerous. It can alert a brute that a victim is in the neighborhood.

—Maya Angelou

One of the boys' first coaches taught a valuable baseball lesson on the first day of practice. He said, "OK, gentlemen [note: the oldest 'gentleman' on the team was six], the first rule on our team is *no whining.*" He said it three times to make sure everyone understood. Throughout the year he was famous for holding up one finger, looking at a whiny player, and asking, "What's rule number one?"

I found out that this wisdom extended to the coach's teenage son, who played on another team in one of the upper levels in our league. The teenager came over just before one of our games started, as his dad was filling out the lineup card. The son started talking about his game that day, including a laundry list of things his coach and the umpire had done wrong and complaints about the scrape he got on his chest when diving back to first. His dad looked up at him, looked at the abrasion, and said, "No whining. It's rule number one." For all I know that was rule number one at their house for everything. If it wasn't, it wouldn't have been a bad place to start.

So when I coached, I remembered the no-whining lesson. It surprised me that as the players got older, their capacity for whining didn't decrease. If anything, as their vocabularies and hormones expanded, it increased along with them. The words got bigger, the concepts got more complex, but in reality, whining at age six that there is a rock in your cleats is the same as whining at age twelve that the umpire doesn't fully understand the infield fly rule.

Played correctly, baseball gives a kid permission to do a lot of things that are otherwise off the list. Standing out in the rain for half an hour in clothes that have to be laundered is generally a no-no. Your baseball coach might actually order you to do so. Don't whine about it.

If you get a special set of clothes dirty, you might be in big trouble at home. A baseball uniform (and glove) is made to get dirty. Think about it—after years of admonitions about keeping your clothes and shoes clean and staying out of the dirt and mud, here is an adult who actually demands that you practice sliding in the dirt and rolling on the grass. How cool is that? Don't whine about it.

Sliding, for example, looks like a lot of fun. Properly done, it usually doesn't hurt, or only hurts momentarily. Improperly done, and from time to time even when done well, it can raise strawberries on your butt, cause abrasions on your hands and cuts to your legs, and get you slapped in the ribs with a leather-covered ball. You'll probably even eventually spike yourself in the leg if you run the bases hard enough. You do not get to whine about it.

My favorite baseball interviews are the ones where the reporter asks a player about an obvious injustice on the field—a bad safe/out call, a home run that didn't count because the umpire couldn't tell if it hit the yellow line, a line drive that may have been caught but probably got trapped by a sliding outfielder. You can tell a lot about the character of a player and the attitude of a team at those times. The whiny ones, the ones who say the umpire has it in for them or the manager called the wrong play, are not my favorites. I like the players who say, "Well, that's the way it goes," or better yet, "We had lots of scoring opportunities early; it shouldn't have mattered what the ruling was on the line drive."

Those players know about rule number one, and they are the kind of players most coaches and managers want on a team. Whining is a habit and a hard one to break. You can bet that a player who constantly whines about the events in a game is also whining about a lot of events in his life.

Unfortunately, there are a lot of grownups out there these days who apparently have never learned this rule. You hear it every day—people whine about their jobs, they whine about their spouses, they whine about the traffic on the way home.

Aside from just being generally obnoxious and unproductive, whining shows a lack of appreciation for the blessings that most of us enjoy. Whining about your commute shows a genuine lack of appreciation for the fact that you have a job and access to transportation to get you there. If your job is so lousy that you spend significant portions of your life telling other people what is wrong with it, then either find a way to fix the problem or find a new job. Stop whining.

Lesson #28
Some Days You're the Bat, Some Days You're the Ball

Sometimes you're the Louisville Slugger, sometimes you're the ball. Sometimes it all comes together, sometimes you're gonna lose it all.
—Mary Chapin Carpenter

I'm less than certain that this whole chapter can sum things up any better than Ms. Carpenter's lyrics do. Some days, everything just seems to go right. Then there are other days. It doesn't matter if you call it fate, or karma, or luck, or just life. The simple fact is that sometimes you have good days and sometimes you have bad days.

Even the youngest Tee Ball players come into the league already knowing this. The life lesson from baseball is not that good days come and bad days come. It's recognizing that you need to enjoy the good days and not suffer too much on the bad days, because neither condition is permanent.

Everyone who has watched much baseball has seen a player who, for whatever reason, just seems to be living a charmed life. I don't just mean that preparation has met opportunity, either. We call it "lucky" when the hitter rips a low line drive back to the box and the pitcher blindly sticks his glove hand out behind him and the ball not only hits it but sticks in the pocket like it was a rosin bag.

Sure, the pitcher has developed excellent reflexes over the years, was alert enough to try to make the play, and had himself in at least a decent fielding position through diligent practice.

The laws of physics say that the ball and his glove both had to be somewhere in space at that particular time. Getting that catch done once in a game may not be lucky—the "residue of design," as Branch Rickey said. It may be skill.

Luck is when the pitcher does that twice, and the wind blows a towering fly ball just past the foul pole, and the fastest runner on the other team stumbles and falls while trying to steal second, all in one day. Just to make it interesting, a guy like that will also throw his bat at the ball in the eighth and it will skip between the first and second basemen as if he meant to do it. The really amazing thing about this is that although it doesn't happen every day, it happens frequently enough that no one makes a big deal out of it.

As there is always a left field to balance out right field, bad days come along to balance out the good. Again, this is more than hitting the ball hard in four trips to the plate with nothing to show for it. It's having a bug fly in your ear on a three/two pitch in the same game where you drop an easy fly ball and where you knock another one from foul territory to fair territory and the other team's worst hitter and fastest runner gets on base.

Another part of this lesson is that it is not just individuals who seem to have good and bad days. Often, entire teams can suddenly wind up in a situation where everything, or nothing, seems to happen right. It's just uglier than a spitball when the cursed team runs into the charmed team on the same day. It would be easy to give illustrations from the youth league diamond—teams explode and implode there every spring all over the country. It's more effective, though, to think about big league teams who have experienced Murphy's Law for nine whole innings.

In 2004 the New York Yankees played the Cleveland Indians. It was the last beautiful afternoon of August in the Bronx—a high of eighty-two degrees, sunny, with a light breeze. It was, however, not a beautiful day for the Yankees or the 52,000 Yankee fans who crowded into the "house that Ruth built." Two short weeks before, the Yankees had been in first place in the East by more than ten games and cruising toward another playoff appearance. Cleveland, on the other hand, was a .500 ball club that hadn't won a game at Yankee Stadium since 2001. Making the playoffs was an outside chance for the Indians, at best.

Things seemed to start off innocently enough. Cleveland's leadoff hitter lifted a lazy fly ball to centerfield. Their second hitter singled cleanly to right centerfield. That's when things started to get strange. Yankee pitcher Javier Vazquez (who had already won thirteen games that year) got the ground ball on the infield from Cleveland's third hitter, Matt Lawton. The hit was too slow for a double play. The Yankees' dependable second baseman, Miguel Cairo, decided that rather than throwing the ball to first to get Lawton out easily, he would try to get the lead runner at second. His throw was late.

Suddenly, not only did the Yankees not get the double play to end the Indians' at bat, they didn't get any outs. So instead of two out and one on, there were now two runners on and only one out. The Indians' cleanup hitter, Victor Martinez, walked. Now the bases were loaded. Travis Haffner tripled to centerfield, and things turned ugly.

Cleveland scored three runs in each of the first three innings. They scored six in the fifth inning and six more in the ninth. The final score was 22-0. Omar Vizquel of Cleveland had six hits—a good week for some players. It was the biggest shutout victory in Major League Baseball in over one hundred years. It was the worst loss the Yankees had suffered in their entire history. The instructive part is how the team reacted to the game.

Various Yankee players referred to the game as embarrassing.

And it was. But having one bad day in August was not the end of the season for the Yankees. Alex Rodriguez probably summed it up best when he said, "It's one game. If we win 22-0 we don't get credit for three victories." In fact, the Yankees bounced back to beat Cleveland each of the next two games.

Whether it's an individual or a team, good and bad days on the diamond extend to good and bad days in the wider world. Baseball gives you lots of chances to be both the bat and the ball—just like life. Some days the algebra professor will misread your answer sheet and give you eight extra points on the final exam, and on the same day you'll find twenty dollars in the pocket of the jacket you haven't had on in months, and the motorcycle cop will be looking the other way when you scoot through the intersection after making less than a full stop at the stop sign.

There'll be the other kind of days, too, days that the alarm doesn't go off and you're late for work, and the conference call starts ten minutes early, and you spill coffee on the new shirt your spouse gave you.

The trick is what to do. It's a simple lesson in the abstract but somewhat harder in the real world. First, don't get too far down on the bad days. You have to learn not to fear the days where it just doesn't all come together and not to complain that those days seem to occur too often. Otherwise you get so discouraged, depressed, and disappointed that you start seeing only the bad days and missing those days where it all works right.

Learn that there are days when everything falls into place, as though you threw a jigsaw puzzle up in the air and it fell on the card table with every piece locked together perfectly. You won't have a day like this every day. Things even out at some point. Knowing that, you have to learn to celebrate the days when it all comes together, without worrying about those days when it does not.

Lesson #27
Respect for Authority

Unthinking respect for authority is the greatest enemy of truth.
—Albert Einstein

I really hate the expression "You're not the boss of me" that was in vogue awhile back. For a short while, the phrase had some positive influence as an option to avoid negative peer pressure. However, the law of unintended consequences took over, and it wasn't long till the phrase had mutated into "No one is the boss of me." The idea of going through life with no one to answer to resonates especially well with the average seventh grader.

A few people have the luck, money, and personality to live happily and successfully without oversight or guidance. Most people have a boss to whom they must answer. In fact, most people answer to more than one boss, and they can generally name the individuals to whom their bosses answer. In reality, living your life without anyone in a position of authority over you is extraordinarily unusual. This baseball lesson is learning how to deal with those who do have authority over you.

Kids are used to people telling them what to do. Parents, teachers, Sunday-school leaders, older siblings, relatives of various other stripes—all play a big role in the life of a child. Baseball adds new individuals to the mix.

Sure, when the fourth-grade math teacher really, really wants the class to learn the multiplication tables, that teacher will go to great lengths to help the children. However, you aren't going to find all that many kids who are excited about learning that 6x7=42. Even after they know the facts cold, taking a multiplication test is more like enduring a visit from Aunt Mildred than it is like stealing second.

A baseball coach is a new individual who wants to help the players be the best players they can be. A good coach will want the players to play better than they think they can, partly for the good of each player, but also for the good of the team. This is different from the schoolteacher. Either way, though, it makes it easier to learn the rules for dealing with the boss, whomever that happens to be, if you know that the boss has your improvement at heart. If what you are learning to do is fun, that's even better.

The rules you really need to get along with the boss are usually pretty simple: be respectful, follow directions, try hard. You won't succeed at every job just because you do these things, but you won't fail at any because you do these things consistently. Also, if you manage to do all these things, the boss is more likely to look around to find something better you can do because, for some reason, these traits are becoming scarce.

- *Be respectful.* Treating the coach respectfully when you are a player will get you noticed. All the good baseball coaches (and managers) I have watched have earned the respect of their players. Good bosses in other professions do the same thing. Start out assuming that the coach deserves your respect. You don't have to be intimidated—just treat the coach as if he is in charge and deserves to be because, well, because he is. Having a respectful attitude is likely to make the coach be respectful of you. (If he is not, you can deal with that and then move along when you can. That disrespect does not give you the green light to be disrespectful in return—it gives you the green light to find another place to play.) I put respect first for this reason: if you follow directions and work hard but still have a lousy attitude, nobody will want to work with you because of that attitude.

- *Follow directions.* Baseball is a great tool for learning to follow directions. Everything from the physical technique for playing positions and hitting to getting the steal sign requires you to follow directions. Like a lot of other things, learning baseball technique is a never-ending process. The oldest veterans on the team still take batting practice in front of a hitting coach. The most skilled pitchers in the big leagues still show up to spring training before position players, just to work on technique with the coaches. Learning the knack of following orders, dealing with a long list of things to do, judging priorities, and deciphering occasionally conflicting instructions will make you a good shortstop, and it can also make you a good plumber. It doesn't really matter how hard you try—if you are not following the directions, your effort is just wasted.

- *Try hard.* People notice if you are doing the best you can. Most of the time, if you try hard enough, you will succeed. Sometimes you won't. However, if you have a reputation of trying hard, following the directions you are given, and having a respectful attitude while you do it, you probably won't be penalized when you can't do something. On top of that, you will gradually find that there are a lot of goof-offs in the world. If you try hard, you'll at least get ahead of all of them.

Baseball also teaches you how to deal with a series of bosses at the same time. Every player has a lot of bosses at one time—parents, the head coach, the base coach, the coach in the dugout who tells everyone to sit down and shut up, the umpires, the team leaders who have been in the league longer. . . . They all have different bosses, too.

The average student may have heard that the teacher reports to the principal at school, but without much concept for what that means. A baseball team illustrates this clearly.

Beyond the hierarchy concept, baseball will also teach that the boss is not always right. A player who is paying attention can learn how to appropriately question authority—not just to be contrary or challenging, but in constructive ways that work for everyone's benefit. Most professional baseball manager/umpire arguments you see are all about theater. Some of the older guys used to get genuinely upset, I think. Earl Weaver (who was once thrown out of a game during the exchange of lineup cards at home plate) and Billy Martin come to mind.

These days, I think managers mostly yell at umpires to energize the team, protect players who didn't like a call, etc. In youth baseball, however, you see a number of arguments where a coach is genuinely interested in a rules interpretation, or changing a call not because he disagrees with whether the tag was made but because a (usually) youthful umpire may not quite have understood all that just happened.

I've seen and participated in discussions like this. Even an experienced umpire may have trouble with a quick interpretation of a complicated rule (e.g., how does the infield fly rule apply if a runner advances on an infield fly ball not caught and knocked foul by the infielder standing in fair territory?). Coaches who come sailing out of the dugout red in the face, yelling at a fifteen-year-old umpire as if he just keyed the coach's car, are likely to get nowhere, as they are mostly showing off their own immaturity.

The same rules for dealing with bosses get you where you need to be when you challenge authority, like that of the umpire. Be respectful, follow the league's directions for challenging calls, and try hard to explain unemotionally why you think things need to be changed. At least you will get to have your say. Most kids know that what goes in the big leagues does not work at the city park fields. It would be nice if all youth coaches remembered it, too.

Young players can also learn that being respectful and following instructions does not mean blind adherence to a silly or wrong instruction. Marc played shortstop on a six-year-old team. He once fielded a ground ball with a runner on third and just held it.

The coach screamed, "Throw it to first." His dad screamed, "Throw it to first." The fans screamed, "Throw it to first."

Marc yelled back, "I can't. He doesn't know how to catch it."

Perhaps that's an extreme example. But Marc knew if he threw it to first, a run would score. If he held it, maybe the next hitter would strike out. I have seen older players politely and respectfully explain to a coach why a particular plan wouldn't work. I have been on the receiving end of good advice myself. This is particularly true when the kids know their opponents better than the coaches do.

Kids on my teams found out soon enough that standing in front of the coach between innings, begging and yelling for a chance to play first base, was a quick route to an inning off or an inning in left field. Kids who caught up to me during warm-ups, or stayed after a game to tell me they wanted an opportunity, usually got it next time out.

Carefully and unemotionally explaining to your boss why it's a lousy idea to ship blown glass without packing Styrofoam peanuts around it will get you a lot farther than calling him an idiot and stomping off to the loading dock. Knowing how to deal with authority includes knowing when and how to question it. Learning it in baseball enables you to do it wrong without big penalties and, at least at the youth level, teaches that sometimes that is effective.

Lesson #26
How to Deal with Different Kinds of People

You must look into people, as well as at them.
—Lord Chesterfield

Up to a certain age it's important for children to think that the whole world is made up of trustworthy people who love them, will help take care of them, and are in many respects all alike, at least as far as the child is concerned. Someday, though, children have to learn that not everyone is just like them and, sad though it is, not everyone in the world will have their best interests at heart.

To the occasional consternation of the local baseball league, we pretty much insisted on our kids having different coaches, season after season. After a certain point, there weren't enough teams and different coaches to make this come true, but by then I had achieved a secret baseball goal, or at least I had tried. I wanted the boys to learn that the world is full of lots of different types of people as well as how to get along with them.

Different baseball coaches made for good examples. The boys had good coaches and bad coaches (please understand, I don't think the boys ever had any evil coaches, just some who were better at dealing with kids than others and some who were better at teaching baseball than others).

Some coaches like to yell. Some coaches are quiet. Some coaches drill fundamentals with the same three drills the whole season. Some coaches make up funny little games to play at practice instead. Some coaches threaten, while others are such big cheerleaders they might as well have megaphones and pompoms. Last year's coach might pick you up and hug you for a meaningless first inning base on balls. This year's coach might just say "nice hit" if you slam a walk-off dinger with two outs. All those different styles do not necessarily mean one coach is right and another coach is wrong. It's just that people—and coaches—are different.

I'm trying to teach two ideas here. First, all through life you are going to have different teachers, bosses, supervisors, customers, club presidents, etc., and they are all going to have different ways of doing things. It's important to learn how to deal with lots of different kinds of personalities. When you eventually learn to say, "Oh, the boss didn't congratulate me for selling the most life insurance policies of anybody for the last two years, but that's just how he is" (so long as that's the truth), you are learning how to make your life a lot easier. Probably, you will also learn that when that boss congratulates everyone but you, it might be time to take a long look at changing jobs.

Second, you can learn skills that you can apply in your own life from watching how different people work. Be the kind of coach that you'd like to play for. If you don't like it when a coach yells at you all the time, remember that when it's your turn to run a drill.

As you might suspect, there's a third facet of this lesson, too. Some people are jerks. This is certainly one of the less fun things that parents someday have to tell their children. Rotten people show up in baseball, even youth league baseball, in about the same proportion as jerks turn up in all endeavors. I'm sure there are rotten forklift drivers, legislators, and advertising executives just as there are rotten coaches, third basemen, and fund-raising candy sales chairmen.

It would be a fine world if everyone played nicely in the sandbox. If you've ever been in a sandbox, you know better. Kids find out early on that some people aren't nice and aren't to be trusted and that it's hard to go anywhere for long without running into one of them. What is useful is remembering that not everyone in the world is going to be nice to you all the time. Some of them will not have a particular reason for being nasty—it's just the way they have chosen to be. What is even more useful is learning how to deal with these "cracked bats" when you do run across them.

Frankly, however, most of our experience with rotten individuals came not from coaches, but from players' parents and, especially, other players. Sure, some coaches favored their own kids, were rude to less talented players, or manipulated the rules to try to "help" their team. And we knew a lot more players who liked to come in with their spikes high, caused trouble in the dugout, and ended up taking an inordinate amount of the coach's time. Just like an adult, a child must learn how to spot these types and how to deal with them once they are identified.

The good news for me as a dad was that I got to teach some object lessons, but for the most part my boys figured out their own strategies for handling the jerks. This is the way it usually works. All children have to learn these coping skills. I'm sure many learn the skills in daycare or at school, or perhaps at the neighborhood playground. You will learn those skills playing baseball. If you already know them, you can hone them.

I used to tell parents before the season started, "I don't know most of the kids here. You do. Be honest with them and yourselves. If your child tends to act up sometimes, to irritate others, or otherwise make a nuisance of himself, please warn him to keep that under control at baseball. I won't be able to watch every player every minute, no matter how much I'd like to.

"At first, kids will all tolerate a little guff from each other. As they get used to each other, as the weather turns hotter and the pressure of the season builds, that natural tolerance will begin to wear off. When it is completely gone, remember that these kids are going to be more or less trapped in a steel cage with each other, armed with spiked shoes and clubs that I am teaching them to swing. Please tell your kids to be careful and respectful of each other."

Given long enough, you can probably come up with a few solitary careers or life choices where human interaction is way down the list (e.g., firewatcher). But most aspects of life—academic, career, and social—involve dealing with other people. Sometimes those people are a lot like you and easy to get along with; sometimes they aren't. Learning how to deal with the different sorts of people you run into is essential.

Lesson #25
Control Your Emotions

There's no crying in baseball.
  —Tom Hanks, as Jimmy Duggan in *A League of Their Own*

People blow their tops, lose their temper, freak out, go nuts, crash and burn, burst out crying, scream blue murder, yell their heads off . . . you get the idea. If you are going to be a good baseball player, or good at anything else, you have to learn to control your emotions. Before you finish this chapter, note that it is not subtitled "Big Boys Don't Cry."

By "control" your emotions, I don't just mean not losing it. Partly, I do mean that you have to keep your emotions in check; don't let everyone know, by your actions, what you think or how you feel. But by "control" I also mean that you need to channel the energy that you would waste in one of the activities listed above into something that helps both you and your team. Unfortunately, as far as I know, the only way to learn to control your emotions is to lose control of them a few times. I suppose it is true that sometimes the only way to know where the line is marked is to cross over it and look back. Baseball guarantees to give you the chance to do that. Here's why.

Baseball is a difficult game to play well. When the pressure builds because the game is close or the other team has put their best player into a good situation, it becomes harder to play well. If you let your emotions master you, then you will make mistakes, sometimes critical ones. Controlling emotion both by keeping it in check and channeling it into better efforts is key.

It is hard on a young shortstop if he knows that the other team's best hitter is up and frequently hits to the left side of the infield. When the shortstop knows, from watching the catcher's sign, that the next pitch will make it more likely the batter will hit his way, he may get nervous or excited. If the shortstop gets nervous and emotional, he may lose track of the game situation. He may forget to cover second if a runner on first steals, he may lose track of his responsibility if the hitter surprises everyone with a bunt, or he may get so excited when he gets a chance to field that he commits an error.

You have to find a way to master your emotions to let your muscles do what you have trained them to do. Unfortunately, controlling emotions belongs in the easier-said-than-done category.

The average player will have dozens of chances over a regular season to either master his emotions or to let his emotions master him. You occasionally see players at the big league level who look as though they play on raw emotion all the time—pumping their fists, yelling, slapping their thighs with their gloves. Don't be fooled. It takes some emotion to play baseball and the better players know that. However, at the major league level many players are also entertainers and view themselves that way. When the time comes for those players to control their emotions and do their job, they quickly calm down and concentrate.

Randy Johnson pitches with a lot of visible emotion. If you watch as he takes the sign from the catcher and focuses on the spot where he wishes to place the ball, you won't see him yelling or screaming. His eyes lock on target, he controls his breathing, and he controls his emotions until the play is complete. Then he's back to celebrating a strikeout.

I'm not saying it's all an act with Johnson; in fact, I doubt that it is. I am saying that he possesses a very valuable baseball skill, the skill to control his emotions and channel the energy those emotions would otherwise use. Besides that, Johnson is an exception that proves the rule.

You would have a difficult time guessing the game situation if you could only see the faces of pitchers like Greg Maddux or Tom Glavine. Up by five with two out in the sixth produces the same expression as a bases loaded, full count pitch in the bottom of the ninth. Sure, you'll see a swear word or a glove slapped if a pitch doesn't go just as intended, but not on the mound, not when it's time to pitch.

As I discuss elsewhere, hitting a baseball is a hard thing to do. It drives me crazy when parents and coaches yell at players to "get mad at the ball." If a hitter should happen to rip one after this instruction, a lot of good things may have happened, but wasting energy getting mad at the ball wasn't one of them.

A "mad" player—that is, one controlled by his feelings instead of his technique and ability—will squeeze the bat handle as if he's trying to choke it to death. A mad batter will tense his shoulders and trap his elbows against his ribs. In a hurry to get to the ball, a mad batter will begin moving long before the pitcher begins his delivery, typically overstride, jerk his head out and up, and take a mighty off-balance cut.

Occasionally, he will coincidentally get his bat at the same point in space as the baseball. Often, though, he will simply rip through the air above the ball, spin around, and perhaps fall on his bottom. Now he's mad at the ball, embarrassed, and frustrated with whoever gave him the instruction to get mad in the first place. The pitcher has to control his emotion not to giggle before he throws an off-speed pitch to finish the poor hitter off.

A batter, more than any other player, needs to be calm and clinical about what he is called upon to do. Raging emotions—anger, fear, anxiety—are his enemies. Nothing will ratchet up emotion like standing in the on-deck circle with the game on the line. Forced to stand there and watch his teammate at bat, he will feel the pressure start to build.

The pressure increases while the catcher and pitcher confer. The hitter might foul off three/two pitches for what seems like forever. It is interesting to try to guess how a player is feeling as he comes to the plate. Sometimes you can tell by watching—he drags his bat and it's all he can do to get it as high as his shoulder. Sometimes he is so sure he can hit whatever the pitcher throws that he seems to skip to the batter's box, twirling his bat like a drum majorette. I always liked the player who made me guess what he was feeling, or if he was feeling anything at all, because he was making the pitcher guess, too.

Losing your emotional control can cost you in a variety of ways. Be the pitcher who gets mad and shows up the plate umpire, and the strike zone will suddenly get so small you couldn't throw a golf ball through it from three feet away. Slinging a bat or a helmet will earn you a chewing out by the coach, and that will invariably be worse than whatever got you upset in the first place.

The advantage of emotion is that it gives you the chance to create some internal energy. If you manage to channel that energy, focus it, in a disciplined manner to the task at hand, you have manufactured an advantage for yourself. If you are upset at an umpire's call on your last pitch, turn the resentment you feel toward him into a determination that the next pitch will have the velocity and placement to make the hitter swing and miss.

If you are nervous that the hitter is going to hit a screaming liner right at you, let that nervous energy allow you to place yourself in the best fielding position possible, to concentrate on the pitch, and to let your body react the way you have trained it. In short, don't let your mind prevent your body from doing its job.

Different players do different things to control their emotions, and often a kid will need to discover for himself what technique is effective. As a parent or coach, about the best you can do is explain the idea of controlling emotions. For many players, it takes going through the same routine before every pitch or at bat. For some, it's as simple as taking a deep breath and focusing on what is happening now, not the last inning or the last at bat, or even the last pitch.

Sometimes, of course, a player just needs to let a little emotion out of his system. Finding an acceptable way to do this is a life skill. Cursing at an umpire won't do; throwing your Powerade bottle into the trashcan as hard as you can might. Slinging your bat after a weak grounder to third is not the answer; running all the way to first base as though your life depended on it makes you a gamer.

Outside of the white lines, you have to learn the same control. Many who can't control their emotions end up lonely, in prison, or worse. The driver who has no emotional control behind the wheel of a car is a hazard to himself and others. An adult who hasn't learned when to shut up might call the motorcycle cop a "strutting bag of . . . " and possibly end up behind bars for the evening.

A boy who learns to stand patiently in the on-deck circle with the bases loaded for a two-out turn to bat will be just fine waiting on his first job interview. A pitcher who knows how to react when the umpire has just called strike three, ball three, will be fine when he gets cut off in traffic by a careless bonehead. Even the kid who has learned when and how it is appropriate to "blow your stack" at someone will respond appropriately when the college professor accuses him of missing too much class when the professor actually means the student sitting next to him.

So don't get mad at the ball and don't get mad at the pitcher. Take a deep breath and channel that anger and apprehension into concentration and control. Line up your knuckles, keep your head still, and when that curve ball hangs in the middle of the plate, let the pitcher get mad when you rip it back through the box like a bolt of lightning on a July afternoon.

Lesson #24
Math Counts

The essence of mathematics is not to make simple things complicated, but to make complicated things simple.

—Stan Gudder

It's not a particularly big secret that most kids don't like math. Apparently, this is more true in America than other parts of the world. I find that interesting but not terribly mysterious. Math is exacting and precise. Face it, it's always nicer to get credit for getting close than having to hit the target every single time. Various education experts have cast about for ways to interest kids in math by showing its relevance to everyday life.

I remember "word problems" from when I was in school many years ago, and I have read some of the same type of problems they hand out today. It's really not relevant to a kid's life to ask how long it takes to drive from city A to city B at a given speed. Updating to make the questions seem "cool" and modern by changing it from driving between Altoona and Poughkeepsie to flying a spaceship between the planets Abalone and Zircon is a good instinct but isn't the solution, either.

I have a theory on this. The people who are charged with teaching math, and especially those who write math textbooks, are all good at and have probably always liked math. They are trying to teach their favorite subject to students who would just as soon run twenty gassers than learn how to divide fractions.

I'm confident that the math whizzes understand this problem. However, I fear they want to solve it by trying to get on a kid's level and instilling their love of the discipline in that same kid. That is, on the whole, too ambitious.

The kids who will grow to like math are going to do so. The kids who don't have a natural facility for it are not going to be persuaded to the contrary, even if you let J. K. Rowling write the word problems.

I don't find it a bit mysterious that these two groups aren't communicating very well. Ask any youth league coach—there's no time wasted like the time you waste trying to interest a kid who hates the game. It would be nice to say otherwise (and I'm sure some do), but I don't think it matters to the students how much the teacher loves it.

I don't pretend to have an answer that will work for everyone, but at our house, we dealt with the "math doesn't have anything to do with real life" position not by talking about engineers building bridges or space stations, but by talking about baseball instead.

Early in his academic career, my older son told me the only math you need to know to run a baseball team is to be able to count to nine. At that point, I knew I had him where I wanted him. All it took was finding the right questions to ask. What if you manage an American League team? You'll have to count to ten, won't you? Won't you need to count to at least twenty-six to make sure you have a full roster? A starter might get hurt, you know. How will you know which pitcher to start? Wouldn't you like to take at least a peek at his ERA? You'd better understand fractions and division to do that. What about batting averages? On-base percentage? Slugging percentage? Fielding percentage? WHIP? If you can't do math up to the level of algebra, you are dangerously weak on the knowledge you need to run a baseball team.

I have read that some teams now calculate everything, down to how many runs they'll score and errors they'll make over an entire season, even before the first game of the year. They get amazingly close. Baseball is a numbers game. Besides, just not liking to do something does not mean it isn't valuable.

I guess that's a big part of this lesson. You rarely run into a catcher who enjoys learning to block the ball in the dirt with his body rather than catching it in his mitt. Someday when the speediest kid on the other team has a big lead at third and the pitcher is getting tired, that catcher will be glad he learned that skill. Math is the same way.

If you really want to understand baseball, you'll learn geometry as well. Baseball is a game of arcs, lines, angles, and intersections. If you are really serious about it, you'll read a fascinating little book called *The Physics of Baseball*. (I know that, technically, physics is considered a science class; however, anyone who has taken it knows that it's really just a math class masquerading as science.)

Yes, math is exacting—that's the whole point. Math can be difficult. It can also provide a wide-open window to understand things about the world, to compare things that are otherwise incomparable. In short, it's a lot like baseball itself.

Math counts. Learn it. It will be easier than hitting a curve ball.

Lesson #23
Bridging the Generation Gap

As is the generation of leaves, so is that of humanity.
So one generation of men will grow while another dies.
—Homer, *The Iliad*

In the world of debates, baseball probably inspires as much good-natured (and not so good-natured), esoteric argument as anything you can name. Walk into a bar somewhere—not even in a major league city—look around for the guy in the ball cap, and say something out loud like, "Bob Gibson was a better pitcher than Randy Johnson ever thought about being." If you don't get punched in the mouth, you're probably in for lively discussion the rest of the evening.

With the right group, nothing is too obscure for carefully reasoned analysis. "Do you think the taller mound would have helped Johnson?" This won't work, of course, for every conversational subject. Can you just imagine if someone said something like, "Harry Truman would have campaigned Bill Clinton into the dirt"? People would think you were crazy. Mention that Barry Bonds couldn't hit Walter Johnson's pitches, and you'll make new friends and new enemies faster than you can say "Cy Young."

The truth is that most of these arguments have no rational ending and no "winner" or "loser." Rarely does anyone change their opinion. In some respects, it would be disappointing if many of them came to a complete conclusion. I guarantee you that there are men who read the first paragraph of this chapter and seriously began to mull over the Gibson statement. (This usually causes your girlfriend or wife to say, "Honey, what are you thinking?" It's no use telling her because she won't believe you.)

One thing I love about these endless (some might say fruitless) arguments is the way they carry on from generation to generation. People who never saw Ty Cobb play, which amounts to almost everyone alive now, still read his statistics, look at the photographs, and like to imagine what he could do if he were still around. It doesn't matter how old you are. You are fully entitled to your opinion on Cobb because ten-year-olds can read the same statistics as their grandparents and have the same frame of reference about Cobb.

I liked it when my kids started talking to their baseball coaches about baseball. Most conversations instigated by adults, especially with younger kids, are of the "how old are you?" and "where do you go to school?" variety. After that, things bog down. Kids get uncomfortable, adults get bored, and that's the end of that. Baseball, however, reaches across the generations.

I can remember one of my kids arguing (respectfully) with his coach about the batting order of two other kids on the team. He was seven years old. As I started to call him down, I realized the coach was listening to him quite seriously, so I decided not to interrupt. After the game, I told the coach to tell my kid to shut up anytime he was tired of getting baseball advice. The coach looked surprised. He said, "If I could have eleven minds thinking like that every day, we'd beat every team in the league."

Then I realized another valuable thing my boys could learn from baseball—how to talk to adults. In case you've forgotten, being a kid can be hard work. There's lots to learn and even well-meaning adults can tend to gloss over you. Knowing even a little bit about baseball gave both my boys a chance to begin to talk to adults as peers.

Not every adult can relate to discussions about spelling tests. Most don't play video games and don't care about kids' TV shows. Adults who know baseball, however, don't take age into account much when a child wants to know whether he can steal a base on a particular pitcher, or starts talking about his favorite baseball team. It doesn't work with every adult, of course, just the good ones.

Some poor, deprived, unsophisticated adults are not baseball fans. The ones who are, however, make it easy for a child to build confidence talking to adults. Without knowing it, the kids get it. If they learn to talk to adults about baseball, other subjects come within their reach.

The best place for kids to find these adults is in youth baseball. Most of the coaches are at least baseball fans. Most played, some at pretty high levels. Asking the right questions can bring a flood of stories that the adults enjoy telling and the kids enjoy hearing. The kid doesn't have to be a young Bill James, just a little interested and confident enough in what they want to know and do know to be unintimidated.

Knowing how to talk to adults and having adults who are friends who aren't also your relatives is a big lesson. There may be a generation gap among baseball fans, but it doesn't mean they can't communicate. It just means the younger ones think today's players are better than the ones who played in front of their parents and grandparents.

We can live with that one.

Lesson #22
Competing with Your Friends

Bill Maher and I are on against each other, and we're friends. There's no reason to think competition has to be adversarial.

—Jay Leno

Alex had been one of my younger son's best friends since they were both in the second grade. They did not seem terribly similar on the surface, but Alex was a nice kid with great parents, and Patrick said they were friends, so that was good enough for us.

Patrick and Alex were together a lot at school, but they ended up on separate baseball teams in the same league. The first time Patrick's team played Alex's team, Patrick was on the mound in an inning when Alex came to bat. Acting like typical ten-year-old boys, it was difficult for the two of them to keep from laughing during the at bat. Alex hit a ball to shortstop, was thrown out, and they both laughed about that, too. It was all great fun.

Things were decidedly different in the league tournament. Despite the fact that our league ran a double elimination tournament, the strict rules on how many innings each pitcher could pitch made it critically important to stay out of the "losers' bracket."

When Alex was at bat against Patrick in the tournament game, both boys were stone-faced. Patrick threw as hard as he ever had. Alex swung like he was trying to drive it back in Patrick's teeth. Alex swung through a fastball for strike three and walked back to the dugout without looking at the field. This was just as well, because Patrick had walked off behind the mound and was staring at the scoreboard.

"Uh-oh," I thought. "I wonder if these guys will have any trouble getting over this."

Apparently not. Alex and Patrick had classes together up until high school and chose to be roommates on an overnight eighth-grade field trip.

It was at the tournament game that I realized another lesson the boys needed to take out of baseball. The lesson is how to compete with your friends or, more importantly, what to do after you compete with your friends.

I am aware that children, especially boys, compete with each other in all their activities—video games, bike riding, roller skating, etc. In fact, it's hard to think of any activity that two ten-year-old boys can't turn into a contest. The difference is that if you lose a game of horse in the driveway to your pal, only the two of you know about it and you can get another game up right away. If you lose in front of your parents, the other kids on both teams, and to your friend, it will be a little more difficult.

Another way to look at the friend/competitor concept is how baseball handles "trades." Major league players change teams all the time. Making an enemy of someone on another team in May can turn out to be a real problem when you get traded and have the locker next to theirs in August.

Being out in the "real" world, I have found that the life of cutthroat competition and capitalism that I learned about in school—where one business hoped nothing more than that the competition would fold and no one would arise to take their place—sometimes happens. Mostly, though, a somewhat friendlier model is out there.

Sales representatives know each other from trade shows and chance meetings on the road. Competing businesses often don't hate each other. In fact, sometimes competitors help one another in times of crisis. Just because you are competing with someone doesn't mean you can't be their friend, too. You need to be careful—something may happen at your company and you need to ask the competitor for a job someday. Or the competition may buy your employer. There are lots of reasons to try to stay on at least civil terms with the competition. They don't teach you that in school during basic capitalism instruction. You can learn it on the baseball field, though.

Lesson #21
Work Within Your Own Personality

This above all: to thine own self be true.
—William Shakespeare, *Hamlet*

One of the cool things about playing baseball is getting out on the field and imagining you are your favorite baseball player. The photographers who took team pictures in our league for years had a great scam of creating baseball cards with the players' pictures on them. They even got sophisticated enough over the years to start putting statistics on the back of the card—not performance stats, of course, but height, weight, position, etc. One item they included was "favorite player."

It was interesting to look at the kids' cards and see whom they put down as a favorite player. Mostly, even at the very youngest age levels, the kids had a big league favorite. And I knew, because I was a kid once, that when they went out on the field, sometimes that's whom they pretended to be.

You can see them sometimes, kids of all ages. You can just tell he's standing there on the mound and hearing in his head: "Now taking the mound for the Tigers, number five, Johnny Jones. We'll find out what the kid is made of today." And then it happens. The bases are loaded in a one out-one run game, and none other than Tony Gwynn steps to the plate. The pitcher leans in, gets the sign, looks over to third . . . and even though he's ten years old, fifty-five pounds, and four-feet-nothing in his cleats, he suddenly imagines he is the Rocket, or Pedro, or Mariano.

The problem with this posturing, of course, is that try as you might, you never will really imitate Dontrelle Willis. It's not just the physical gifts that a pitcher like Willis has, it's his entire attitude about the game that can't be copied. You can try to throw the ball the way he does, but unless you just coincidentally have a very similar personality, you won't be able to perform or pitch the way he does. That's one reason why, as often as not, the player I described above will hear the announcer's voice in his head say his own name, instead of Curt Shilling.

Everyone has to learn to work within their own personality. You can fool some of the people some of the time, but if you try to pretend to be something you are not, you can be sure the truth about who you are will step into your uniform eventually. The good news for baseball players is that a person who wants to play baseball can generally find a way to make the game work with their own personality. Baseball does require certain basic ingredients (some of which I talk about elsewhere): courage, determination, competitiveness, the ability to forgive yourself, and a good measure of confidence.

If you have those attributes, even in small doses, you can find a way to make your personality work within the game. In your early years, the game might even give you a couple of those. Where players get in trouble is trying to change their personality—be something they are not—in order to play.

Every team needs a few leaders among the players. At almost every level, this tends to be self-selecting. Some players have a capacity for leadership that their teammates and coaches will notice and appreciate. Some of those leaders are noisy and fiery about their leadership and you don't have to search very hard to find them. Others are more technical, repositioning their teammates as a particular baseball scenario comes up. Some lead by example only: staying in shape, getting key hits, diving for line drives to save runs, getting down a sacrifice bunt to help the team.

All of those techniques work and are valuable. What assuredly will not work is a player who isn't by nature a fiery, yelling sort but tries to act out that role. He'll get away with it for a little while, but eventually almost everyone will figure out that it's an act.

Worse is the player who is not a natural leader but is forced into a leadership role. It's not good for the player and not good for the team. I'm often discouraged that the emphasis on leadership (not just in baseball, but also in business, government, volunteer efforts) has reached the level that not being a "leader" has come to have a negative connotation.

Leadership is critical, but so are followers. If you only value the generals, you will find it very difficult to get anyone to storm the beaches, load the artillery, or cook the meals—and just try to run a war without them.

If your personality is highly competitive, boisterous, and convivial, then trying to play the role of the quietly competent, stone-faced stoic is going to work about as well as using your cap for a glove.

On the way home from a game in which our team had endured six innings of domination by one of the best pitchers in the county, my kid said, "Dad, I wish I could be more like Mitch." Now, Mitch was a very good athlete—speedy, handled the bat well, a solid defensive player, as well as an excellent soccer and basketball player. But Mitch had gone 0-3 on the night, and my son had one of his team's three hits. I was confused.

"Why?" I asked. His answer is the genesis of this chapter.

"Because of what happened when Mitch struck out tonight," he said.

"I didn't notice what you mean. Tell me about it." (Our kids' kindergarten teacher, Mrs. King, not only taught our kids well but gave us this valuable phrase, which we are still using all these many years after kindergarten ended.)

"Well, after Mitch struck out, he just turned around and walked back to the dugout. He hung his bat in the bat rack. He put his helmet back in his bat bag. Then he just picked up his glove and his cap and watched Caleb hit."

"Yes. So?"

"When I struck out, I was mad at everyone—Chad [the opposing pitcher], myself, Coach Randy. I came back in and dropped my bat, I slung my empty water bottle into the trashcan, I walked up and down in the dugout till we got to go back in the field...."

There was more. You can imagine. I did not try to explain this object lesson, but I think it soaked in eventually. Mitch's reaction to his strikeout didn't mean he wasn't upset. He's just more reserved. Rob's reaction to his strikeout didn't mean he wasn't a good person or a good player. He is just more demonstrative about his competitiveness.

If Mitch had come into the dugout and thrown something around after a strikeout, I expect the entire game would have come to a screeching halt while everyone looked on in amazement (I imagine it would be like those old E. F. Hutton advertisements). It's just not how Mitch is put together. Likewise, nobody thought about it for two seconds when Rob had his mini-fit in the dugout (OK, except his mother, but there's another issue or two there).

If, in the same at bat, Mitch had smashed one over the 325 sign in right field, Rob would have looked a lot more excited than Mitch when he got to home plate—jumping up and down, yelling, giving a high five to anyone who didn't care if his hand stung. Mitch would have likely smiled, then jogged to the dugout, where he would have put his helmet in his bat bag, picked up his glove and cap, and watched Caleb hit.

Like the world itself, baseball is full of different personality types. Thankfully, all sorts of different types are successful. The real key is figuring out how to make your personality type work in whatever field you are exploring. You may even find a few things you can't do because of your personality. If you are loud, like to hear yourself talk, and are prone to whistling a tune as you go about your business, you will have a tough time being a librarian. If you are bashful, modest, and don't like to be the center of attention, then runway model probably isn't for you.

In those situations where you have few choices—school, for example—you have to find ways to be successful within the bounds of your own individual makeup. Attempting to act like someone (or something) you are not is making your life unnecessarily difficult and may even contribute to failure.

There are competitive CPAs, modest assembly line workers, and quiet priests just as there are calm pitchers, showy shortstops, and modest catchers. Find out how to fit who you are into what you do. Only you can do it, but baseball will give you early lessons in who you are and how to adjust to the needs of the team. The faster you learn this lesson, the sooner you can get busy shaping your world to meet you.

Lesson #20
Perform under Pressure

By "guts" I mean grace under pressure.

—Ernest Hemingway

When two are out and three are on in a one-run game in the bottom of the last inning, and then the count goes full on the hitter, everyone on the field feels the pressure.

The pitcher is under pressure not to walk the batter and send the tying run across the plate. The hitter is under pressure to somehow get at least one run home without giving away his team's last out. The catcher is under pressure not to drop strike three. The runners are pressured to reach the next base safely and keep the game alive on any ball in play. And the fielders are under pressure to make a play on the ball and win the game for their team.

The year that I coached in kid pitch (nine- and ten-year-olds), I was lucky to have a nice group of kids who got along and tried hard for me. I had very few problems. One of my better players was named Phillip. We knew his older brother and parents from another team and I was glad to have him.

Phillip was a respectful child who tried hard every time, played good middle infield, and was the fastest kid on the team. He was a man of few words. Because he could throw accurately from short to first, I decided to try him at pitcher. In practice he did well. So I told him I would pitch him in a game.

His first game, everything was fine. I had a rule of using a pitcher for only two innings in a game. The pitch limit rules were valuable protection for children's arms but as convoluted as the federal tax code. The way to stay clear of them was to use a child for only two innings per game. Even if you had three games in a week, you were safe.

A few games later, I sent Phillip to the mound again. The first inning was no problem for him, three up, three down against the bottom of the other team's batting order. In the second inning against the top of the order, however, things did not go quite as smoothly. Phillip got an out but then gave up a hit. He walked the next batter. Frankly, though, I wasn't watching Phillip closely. He was mostly throwing strikes and that was all I ever asked of nine-year-old pitchers. Our team was scoring runs and paying attention on defense.

It was a beautiful day for baseball—warm and sunny. It was a Saturday not committed to errands and chores but to baseball. The opposing coach was a nice guy, trying to get his team to play hard while mindful that this was a learning experience for a bunch of fourth graders. In short, I was enjoying myself.

Suddenly, the game came to an awkward halt. I realized that Phillip was giving me the secret coach's signal that only the pitchers know: *Coach, come to the mound. I need to talk to you.* I called time and hustled out. I remember the umpire looking at me strangely.

I doubt I will ever forget the sight that awaited me. Before I was halfway to the mound, Phillip was holding the ball up to me in his bare hand. When I got to him, he had tears in his eyes threatening to run down both cheeks. He looked me right in the eye and said, "I never want to do this again. Ever." The pressure had clearly gotten to Phillip.

"I wonder what Tommy Lasorda does when this happens?" I thought to myself. There was no help for it. I took the ball from Phillip and sent him to centerfield to get control of himself. I put Tanner on the mound in Phillip's place. When I got back to the dugout, Coach Greg asked me why I took Phillip out. I didn't really know what to say. The inning ended a few pitches later.

That night, I called Phillip's parents. From talking to my wife and my son who was on the team, I knew that only Phillip and I knew what had happened. I wasn't the kind of coach who dealt with it very much, but if a child cried at baseball, I owed somebody an apology. Phillip's dad had not been at the game, so I described what happened. He said that Phillip had not discussed it with him but that I didn't owe anyone an apology.

In the next game, I played Phillip at shortstop, left field, and second and all seemed right with the world. His dad told me he had talked with Phillip and whatever happened, I should just go along. I agreed.

During warm-ups before the next game, Phillip came up and started to talk to me. As a coach, you find some players who love to visit with you, talking about baseball, school, and just about everything else going on in their young worlds. Phillip was not one of those kids. In fact, this was, as nearly as I could remember, the first time that Phillip had started a conversation with me all season. Phillip looked me in the eye again and said, "Coach, if you need me to pitch, I can pitch."

If a conversation with Phillip was unexpected, this course of discussion was clearly out of literal and proverbial left field. At first I wasn't sure what to say. Sometimes, however, God—who I believe is a big baseball fan—will look down from Heaven and help a coach do the right thing at the right time. So I realized this was a very big moment for Phillip. I took my sunglasses off so I could look Phillip in the eye and said, "Well, Phillip, I think we have it covered today, but next game, I sure could use you."

Phillip stuck out his hand and shook mine. As I say, I will never forget it. The next game, Phillip pitched and did a good job. He even pitched in the playoffs that year. Phillip's pitching was performance under pressure, but so was facing up to me and telling me that he would. He learned a valuable lesson that season, whether he knew it or not.

This could have been the longest chapter in this book. Every baseball game brings pressure to bear on each player, usually more than once or twice in a game. A season is a long series of pressure-filled situations. Some players handle it better than others, but all of them get to experience what performance pressure feels like.

The point is that life itself is a series of pressure situations, whether it is a job interview, driving the carpool home from school in a thunderstorm, or arguing a capital case to a jury. The only way to learn to perform under pressure is to do it. Baseball gives you many chances to learn what the pressure feels like and how to deal with it so the pressure itself does not inhibit your performance. You might as well learn. Life will demand you know how.

Lesson #19
You Can Learn Almost Anything

What we have to learn to do, we learn by doing.

—Aristotle

If you are the radio call-in host of a sports talk show and it's one of those slow periods of the year where there just isn't all that much to talk about, a dependable question to generate three hours of increasingly heated, increasingly irrational discussion is: "What is the hardest thing to do in all of sports?"

As perhaps you have already surmised, I think arguments like these are a waste of, well, everything—time, energy, effort, breath, broadcast channels. Most people simply pick out the hardest aspect of their favorite sport, the one that is the most physically demanding and requires the most concentration, then submit it as the hardest thing to do. As surely as low and outside follows high and tight, no one in these arguments ever gets convinced. No NASCAR fan will ever be persuaded that it is harder to be a boxer than it is to keep turning left.

The only interesting thing about these arguments is that they generally start off with their candidate, say, the number-two sweeper on the Olympic curling team, and compare their candidate's peculiar skill to hitting a baseball. I've always thought that was the end of the argument.

Whatever else they come up with—jump shots, triple axels, sand shots, escaping blitzing linebackers, doing a one-and-a-half something or other in the pike position—the standard against which it is all judged is the ability to hit a pitched baseball.

It is pretty amazing, all things considered. Most major league pitchers now routinely throw fastballs that travel in excess of ninety miles per hour. (They probably always have. We can just dependably measure it now.) It's sixty feet, six inches from the pitching rubber to the back of the plate, and by the time the pitcher stretches and releases the ball, it's probably less than fifty-five feet (or about five feet for Randy Johnson).

I've read lots of earnest calculations about how fast, in milliseconds, a hitter has to make up his mind to swing at a pitch going that fast. The math works out to about .444 seconds, depending on where you assume the pitcher lets go of the ball. That doesn't really mean anything to me. But think about it this way: sometimes the ball goes so fast the hitter's brain is not able to process the visual images fast enough, and instead of gradually growing visibly larger over the entire distance, the ball will suddenly "pop" from about the size of an aspirin tablet to the size of, well, a baseball. The late umpire Ron Luciano referred to this phenomenon as the "Nolan Ryan Exploding Fastball." Even so, Ryan got hit, sometimes very hard.

Just making contact with the ball is no small achievement. Hitting the ball in fair territory is something else again. Hitting it so that you can make it to first base without it being caught in the air or getting it thrown to first base ahead of you should be newsworthy. It sort of is—every sports page in the country reports every hit.

That would be true if you only got fastball after fastball. You don't. Some pitchers who throw a 90-mph ball will throw 65 mph on the next pitch. They will also throw balls that spin, dive, curve, and—despite the laws of physics—rise on the way to the plate.

And, oh yeah, be alert. Sometimes they come straight at you.

Hitting is, however, so common that if a pitcher can keep the other team from doing it for twenty-seven outs in one game, he'll be idolized and celebrated. It only happens a couple of times a year. If you can learn to hit a baseball, at any level, it's an achievement. The amazing thing is that, at every level past Tee Ball, there are more hitters than pitchers. Even in the big leagues, there is much hand-wringing about the shortage of pitching talent.

The point is, if you can learn to contort your body into a hitting stance, face the pitcher when your brain is screaming at you "get out of the way, stupid, that thing is coming right at us and hard," and then hit the darn thing with the bat, you should have a well of confidence as deep as centerfield at the Polo Grounds that you can learn to do other unnatural and confusing things—like chemistry, maybe.

Lesson #18
Toughness

Pain is temporary. Quitting lasts forever.
—Lance Armstrong

Other chapters in this book have discussed what can best be described as "mental toughness." This chapter is about the other kind—plain ol' physical toughness. By toughness, I mean how you react when something hurts and, perhaps more importantly, how you react when you know it's going to hurt in a minute. (By toughness, I don't mean that it won't hurt or that you shouldn't cry.)

We spend an almost unreasonable amount of time protecting our children. If some had their way, we'd stuff all kids in the middle of cotton bales, feed them via sterilized IVs, and send them out into the world at adulthood without the first bump, bruise, or scrape. The only pain they would ever feel is the occasional finger prick for a blood test just to make sure everything is perfect. Maybe that's just the natural contemporary parenting instinct.

If you believe (as I do) that each child is a special gift from God given to you for a particular reason, or set of reasons, then why shouldn't you protect that child from physical pain at all costs? Well, because it's lousy preparation for real life, that's why. It's fine to dream and hope that you can raise children to adulthood without their experiencing a broken bone, skinned knees, or a stitch or two, but it's a lousy parenting policy.

The trick seems to be finding the middle ground between

protecting your children like the fragile treasures that they are and warning them that sometimes you have to tough things out a little bit—and then to show them how that works.

Baseball gives kids a chance to get hurt. Yes, lots of kids get hurt every year playing baseball—everything from abrasions and spike marks to broken limbs and torn ligaments. Sadly, from time to time a child will even lose his life. However, given the total number of innings played by all the kids participating in organized and sandlot baseball, I'd say that baseball is relatively safe. Many more children are hurt in auto accidents, but no one talks about banning car travel. Lots of kids drown, but no one has proposed filling in all the swimming pools.

Don't get me wrong, I'm not saying every kid needs to break his leg and get spiked in the face to be a good person. I'm also not saying kids should be intentionally injured just for the sake of being hurt and getting over it. (In fact, we didn't let either of our kids play peewee football largely because of the injury risk.) I am saying that dealing with a little bumping and bruising is not a disaster. It's a learning opportunity.

That you can be hurt and still survive is a life lesson. Kids get hurt all the time, playing red rover, falling off the steps, running into one another on the playground. Getting hurt in private and running into the house to Mom or Dad, or just closing yourself in the bathroom, is a lot different from getting hurt with a crowd looking on.

Baseball gives you a chance to see what it feels like to get hurt, to get hurt out in public, and to let everyone see how you react. Baseball shows you that you can skin your knee and it's not the end of the world. You can pull a muscle, let it heal, and return to competition. You also learn to draw the critical distinction between being hurt and being injured.

Life, like it or not, is going to hurt occasionally. Sometimes it's just physical, like when the doctor says that suspicious spot on your foot needs to come off, or the dentist says, "OK, you may feel a little pressure now." Sometimes you think it's just emotional, and you find out that emotional things sometimes hurt physically, too—your serious girlfriend will decide she wants to be someone else's serious girlfriend, or most difficult of all, someone you love dies. Reacting appropriately to those things requires mostly mental toughness, but it also requires physical toughness. The world is rough and tumble. Raising a generation that can't handle it when it hurts, inside or out, is a risk we cannot afford.

Sure, it stings—sometimes pretty badly—when you get hit on the thigh by an inside fastball pitched by an unusually large southpaw for the other team. Being tough doesn't mean that it doesn't hurt. Tough doesn't mean that you don't cry. But you know what? It will feel a whole lot better if you rub it for a minute, wipe your tears, trot down to first, wait for just the right moment, and then steal second on that overgrown, inside-pitching, no-control son of a gun.

Lesson #17
100 Percent or Concentrate

Do not dwell in the past; do not dream of the future. Concentrate the mind on the present moment.
—Gautama Siddhartha, the Buddha

Occasionally it's interesting to compare the way different generations of players are told the same things. I used to be told not to "take half a swing." Now hitters are told to "get to 180." It's the same concept, stated differently. Back when I was playing baseball, our coaches used to tell us to "concentrate" or "pay attention." Now I hear phrases like "focus" or "100 percent it." I'd be willing to bet that the men who coached me heard a different phrase that meant the same thing back when they were learning baseball.

The truth is, all those phrases have the same idea behind them. Baseball requires 100 percent of your attention—at least if you intend to play it well. An infielder who is only physically in the "ready" position and willing to charge the ball and throw it as hard as possible to the correct base is not concentrating, not even close.

A good infielder who is concentrating will be ready to do those things but will also be thinking about the number of outs and runners on the bases to know where to throw a ball that comes to him, whether the infield fly rule is in effect, whether he has seen this hitter before and knows his tendencies (mostly pulls the ball, likes to bunt, looking to walk, etc.), what the pitch count is (to know how careful his pitcher will have to be with his next pitch), what the sign is from the catcher (an inside pitch to a good right-handed batter should be hit to the left side of the infield), whether his pitcher is tired and might not make a play he normally would, and which of his teammates might be in need of a backup on a particular play.

That's why I find the "100 percent it" phrase interesting (though I get irritated at coaches who think they are smart guys demanding 110 percent or 1,000 percent). Parents often misunderstand this phrase, and some players do, too. When a coach asks for 100 percent, he's usually not asking for the player to try as hard as he can physically.

Most players give 100 percent physical effort. They try to run as fast as they can, throw as accurately as they can, and hit as hard as they can.

A major difference between the good players and the so-so players (and the good teams and the teams that are just in a hurry to get to snack time) is the amount of mental energy they spend on the game. Spending that mental energy is what concentrating or giving 100 percent really means.

When a base runner breaks from third toward home on a grounder to deep short, very few of them (unless they just don't want to be out there in the first place) run half-speed from third to home, and few shortstops throw the ball less than as hard as they can to cut down the runner.

In the example above, the player on third will run as fast as he possibly can to get home. Competitiveness, adrenaline, a screaming base coach, a desire not to let his teammates down, and pleasing his parents will all combine to push him down the chalk. All that energy, though, amounts to less than a 100 percent effort. The 100 percent effort means that the player was concentrating before the pitch. He knew what he needed to do and when to do it. His head was in the game.

It means he knew there were runners behind him on first and second and he had to run and beat the throw. It means he noticed the pitcher wasn't paying any attention to him and he got an extra step on his lead. It means he wasn't talking to the kids in the dugout, watching the crows make lazy circles over the centerfielder, or scraping up pebbles with his cleats.

It means he knows that the batter, now a runner, is one of the slowest kids in the league, and if he can coax a throw home he might beat it, while the runner heading to first will be thrown out by three steps. It means he knows the shortstop has a strong arm but isn't accurate and has just as much chance of throwing it to the backstop as he does getting it to the catcher. That's concentration. That's giving 100 percent.

In addition to requiring the mental aspect of the game to reach the 100 percent level, there is a time when coaches speak of the physical aspect. It's easy to give 100 percent effort in the top of the first inning with one down and one on. It's a different matter in the bottom of the last inning of a three-run game. At that point, concentration includes not only keeping your mind sharp for the things you may be required to do on the field but also pushing your body harder to give more than you think you have.

The obvious example is a pitcher who may have worked a few more innings or batters than usual. As he tires, the pitcher will tend to lose his mental edge as well as his physical edge. The pitcher who is tired is more likely to make a mistake because of his fatigue. He needs to concentrate on his technique and give 100 percent of his mental and physical effort with each pitch to do his job. Concentrating on what he wants and needs to do with each pitch will give this pitcher a boost and let him do more than he thinks he can.

The world outside of baseball often requires the same thing. The guy making change at the drive-through window and the orthopedic surgeon both have to concentrate to do their best jobs. Learning how to concentrate, give 100 percent, and do it when you are fatigued will make a difference in your life that people—bosses, teachers, customers, colleagues—will all notice and applaud you for.

Learning this skill at baseball and continuing to push yourself to develop it further will make you better at everything you do.

Lesson #16
Don't Waste Your Time on Something You Hate

Is life not a thousand times too short for us to bore ourselves?
—Friedrich Nietzsche

Nothing breaks my heart quite like having to watch a child who obviously and absolutely does not want to play baseball trudge out on the diamond for another few hours of misery. It doesn't happen as often as you might expect, but it does happen and it is sad.

As you know by now, I think of baseball as an elegant pastime. Baseball is a game that is so transcendent that, even when it is played very badly (and I've sat through plenty of that), effort and genuine enthusiasm can overcome the lack of skill and still make the game engaging and exciting.

On the other hand, baseball can be quite ugly. An umpire with a chip on his shoulder or the mistaken idea that even one person in the stands has come to watch him can ruin the best of games.

A manager who has no feel for the rhythm of the game and tries to pull levers and push buttons at every at bat can ruin a game, too. Baseball played without effort and enthusiasm can be as ugly as last season's practice socks. Additionally, it is not only dangerous to the player who loathes it but even to the game itself.

A player who does not want to play is not going to pay attention. Losing focus in a baseball game makes the player a liability for his team's efforts, as well as a safety hazard. It's easy enough to understand—a shortstop who is watching the pretty lady walk her terrier up the sidewalk is running the risk of taking a line drive to the side of his head. If he misplays a ball, his pitcher has to throw more pitches, putting wear and tear on his arm. If he's standing in the base path, the runner from second may collide with him while he's trying to pick up a ball hit in the gap. His outfielder can throw out his arm trying to make the long throw home, because he's forgotten he's the cutoff man.

In addition to the very real physical danger, there is a larger danger to the game. A child who doesn't want to play baseball but is made to is going to wind up hating not only the person who made him play but also the game itself. This grates on my nerves like steel cleats on an aluminum bench. Many kids who were not particularly good at baseball still enjoy watching the game when they are unable to play any longer (I'm raising my hand). Kids who learn to hate baseball by being forced to play are very unlikely to become fans later on or to encourage (or even allow) their children to play the sport. They will spread their distaste.

I suppose there is no end to the list of reasons why parents send kids out to the ballpark who would rather eat a spinach and lima bean casserole than go. The number-one reason, and the cliché, is the frustrated athlete (usually the dad) who was good at baseball but never good enough to suit himself, or was miserably horrible and has decided to remedy his own shortcomings through his kid.

This scenario is real and it does happen, though not nearly so often as the youth league detractors would have you think. Oddly enough, however, some of the best, most enthusiastic young baseball players I have been around fit this very pattern. Sadly, some of the least enthusiastic I have seen also fit this pattern.

I have seen children cry in the dugout to keep from taking the field or stepping up to the plate. To be fair, I have also seen kids cry because they had to sit out an inning or the game ended, even when they won, because they wanted one more turn at bat. But the parents who are trying to live or relive their own baseball dreams through children who don't want to play are bad for the game.

I can understand having a child play one season to find out if they like it. Forcing a second season on an unhappy camper is inexplicable. I suppose if it's the worst parenting mistake ever made, they are hitting for the cycle, but I suspect that a mistake in this arena indicates mistakes in others.

Another primary example of sending a baseball-hating child out to the field is the not-so-well-meaning parent who views youth baseball as a babysitting service. Ask someone who has coached more than one or two recreation league teams, and they will be able to tell you about a kid whose parents mostly dropped them off early (or asked the coach for a ride so they didn't have to leave home) and showed up last to pick them up after the game or practice was all over.

It's one thing for a parent to behave that way when the kid is one of those little dugout rats who can't seem to get enough baseball. For the kid who hates baseball, it is another thing entirely.

Face it, the child knows he's being farmed out. He's not going to like the farm no matter what. Baseball is not the primary issue—attention is. As a coach, there is almost nothing you can do with a kid like this except sit around for the extra half-hour after practices and games, babysitting a child who isn't yours, when you should be home with your own family. This kind of kid is at least as big a hazard as the first kind of kid, because in addition to other ill effects, he sours volunteer coaches on coaching.

We had one of these kids on our team one year. His parents

were divorced. For awhile I fell into the trap of believing that his mom was just overwhelmed trying to raise the child without the father around. That's why she never got to practice on time, came late to retrieve him, and didn't show up to watch his games.

However, about the tenth game of the season, her son finally hit the ball fair, something he had not managed even in practice. When he ran to first base, it was one of the few times all season he didn't have an expression on his face as if he was sitting in a pediatrician's waiting room.

After the inning, I bragged about the child to my assistant coach and said, "Boy, I wish his mom had been here to see that." Greg just looked at me and shook his head as if I had told him that I never believed that Barry Bonds used steroids. He sighed and finally said, "Well, it wouldn't have taken much effort, but she would have had to have stopped making out in the car with her boyfriend out where the parking lot lights are burned out." I still felt sorry for the kid, but that was the last time I was sympathetic to his mother. At least she wasn't late to pick him up that night. He didn't want to play and didn't want to be there.

By the end of the season, he didn't have a friend on the team because he had irritated everyone in the dugout. He needed attention, but not from his teammates, and not from slipping ice down their jerseys while they were watching the game.

Coincidentally, there was a child on the same team who was not a very good player and whose mom was raising him alone. She had him there on time for every game or called in advance to say why he wouldn't be there. He was always geared up, ready to go, and by the time the season started he was genuinely interested in trying to play. I showed him drills he could do at home.

One day I got him to stay a few minutes after practice to try to get him to throw with his whole arm instead of just pushing the ball. I looked up and there stood his mom way out with us in left field, in high heels with a notebook and a pen to take notes, asking if she could learn to help him. I wanted to hug her. She had a date at our last game that year, but she and the date sat in the stands and watched the game. I was proud of him and his mom when he got a hit. He may or may not still be playing, but I'll bet you a hot dog he doesn't hate baseball.

The third example of kids who hate baseball are the ones whose parents make them play due to a misguided sense that Junior needs to get in shape and baseball is the way to do it. Baseball is not a fat farm (oops, I mean rural weight-reduction facility).

Kids who play baseball are in better shape than kids who don't do anything, to be sure. But I've watched the kids who are forced to come to baseball for their health. They goof off during stretching exercises, cut through the outfield during running, and never swing the bat. The only exercise they get is carrying their gear to and from the car.

To add insult to injury, the average youth baseball concession stand is the mother lode for a kid with a craving for calories—candy bars, nachos, hot dogs, colas, and sports drinks abound and the kids all love it. Someone ought to do a study. I'd be willing to bet that a kid who hates baseball but gets dragged to the park ends up gaining weight over the course of a season.

Running halfway to the fence and back and spending three innings standing in right field like a uniformed foul pole won't burn the calories in one half of the Powerade he drank before the game. A kid who likes to play can stay in good shape on the diamond. A kid who hates to play is probably going to end up shaped like a diamond.

After the first year or two, any kid who says he doesn't like baseball probably knows what he is talking about. All his parents' deferred dreams, need for sitting services, and interest in exercise are not going to change that. Some people don't like country music. I don't like Rocky Road ice cream. Some kids don't like baseball.

The first year I was an assistant coach, one of our players showed up for his first baseball practice with his dad, who was cutting tags off his new glove when they arrived. Minnie Pearl meets Satchel Paige.

The kid made it through stretching, running, and learning about the diamond. He even warmed up OK. When he took his first turn at fielding a grounder, the head coach got into the ball a little bit. It took a bad hop on a pebble or something and smacked the kid right in the mouth. It busted both his lips. He walked away and never came back. You know what? I don't blame him one bit. I hope his dad was able to get a refund on the glove.

As a child you have to do lots of things you probably hate for good reasons—going to school (see the chapter on math), having to give smelly old Aunt Imogene a hug at the family reunion, eating a particular green vegetable. Life, especially the childhood part of it, is way too short to invest it in a pastime you hate.

I want my boys to understand that life is too short to spend it doing things you hate, especially things that aren't required. I hope they stop playing if the game becomes tiresome. If their kids play a couple of seasons and say they don't want to go back because they don't like baseball, I hope they don't make them. Find something they do like and let them do that. That's a good general life rule, too. If you are doing something and realize you hate it, find a way to do something else. It turns out that life, like childhood, is short.

Lesson #15
You Can't Do Anything about the Rain

Some days you win; some days you lose; some days it rains.
—Kevin Costner, as Crash Davis in *Bull Durham*

As parents, especially of young children, we have a solid natural instinct to control almost every element of our children's world. For a time, we can almost do it. We get to control food supply, clean diapers, temperature, etc. It is amazing and unsettling how quickly this level of control fades away and it is time for the children to realize that Mom and Dad, as terrific and well intentioned as we are, just don't control the whole world. This is, incidentally, a tough but valuable lesson for Mom and Dad, too.

One good example of this painful truth is that I don't play baseball for a living because I did not have the necessary ability to do so. When they were young, my kids simply could not comprehend this. Dad needs a job, some men play baseball for their job, Dad likes baseball, so . . . Actually, it's hard to argue with the logic of that.

For their part, the boys remained exasperated that I didn't quit my current job and show up in uniform to play first base at Turner Field. (I like their view of the world. Not only do you get to play Major League Baseball just because you want to, but you get to pick which team you play for.) On the other hand, explaining that I do not and have never had the talent to make the average high school baseball team was not going to cut it as an explanation. After all, they said, "you can practice." Why didn't I think of that?

My older son spent the entire year before he was old enough to play in the local youth league anticipating getting to play. We practiced in the backyard, went to see some games, and talked about what really playing with a team would be like. In the fullness of time, we finally attended his first practice on a cloudy, windswept Saturday afternoon in early March.

Unlike many things in life, it was all he dreamed it would be. He had a team, he had Coach Terry to give him instructions, and he got to hit a real pitch with a real bat and run down a real base path to a real first base. Later he got to field ground balls. He got to put on the catcher's equipment and squat down behind the plate. Just before Opening Day, he got a full uniform with a cap. We bought him some cleats. In short, he had died and gone to five-year-old almost heaven. The only thing that remained was to play in an actual game.

And then, it began to rain.

It rained a lot. It rained by the bucketful. It rained with an intensity that might have impressed Noah himself. Opening Day was delayed. Even after baseball started we lived through one of the longest, wettest springs and early summers in the history of our state. The five- and six-year-old Royals had seven rainouts in a seventeen-game schedule.

Once, we drove all the way to the fields on a bright May afternoon, only to see a cloud blow over the pine trees on the western horizon and soak the field as we sat in our car and watched. After about twenty minutes the sun reappeared, but the field looked more appropriate for a bass anglers' event than a baseball game.

After trying to patiently explain all the various factors at work in this disappointment (you do this with a first child), after trying to reason through why we couldn't play indoors, or just stay at the park till the water dried, or buy giant fans to blow on it like we did after the carpet was cleaned . . . we finally retreated to the sad and desolate refuge of the truth.

"Son," we said, "we just can't do anything about the rain." So there it was, out in the open at last at a level even a five-year-old could understand. Mom and Dad aren't, after all, omnipotent. That's a big lesson there.

Eventually this phrase became a part of our regular family vocabulary. It is a metaphor for all the other things that Mom and Dad simply can't control. When our younger son lay down on the floor and cried the night he finally realized the immutable chronological truth that he would never be older than his big brother . . . well, we can't do anything about the rain either.

I suspect that, one day when the kids are grown and have moved away, there will be a time when my wife and I will remind one another that we can't do anything about that rain either.

Lesson #14
Courage

'Tis said that courage is common, but the immense esteem in which it is held proves it to be rare.

—Ralph Waldo Emerson

If you want to feel a little good old-fashioned fear, take the batter's box in a game against an overdeveloped pitcher who is two years older than you are, outweighs you by fifty pounds, has permission to throw a solid object at you as hard as he can . . . and has hit the last three kids who were standing right where you are. Oh, and by the way, your primary job is not to get out of the way but to hit the baseball if Gorilla George happens to throw you a strike.

I know, adults need courage all the time. You have to face the boss and ask for a raise; you think she'll say yes but you have to gather your courage and ask her to marry you; you have to raise your kids. I'll tell you, though, the world that children live in is frightening by degrees adults take for granted on a daily basis. Starting school is a fear-inducing experience. We send kids to movies like *Snow White* and *Harry Potter* without a second thought. For good old-fashioned, knee-buckling, sweaty-palm fear, there's nothing like dragging your bat to the plate in a youth baseball game.

Spend a few minutes thinking about old Gorilla George. You are eight years old. It is hot. You are just learning to hit pitches. Now, it is late in the game. Three men are on base. Two of them have new bruises—the "lucky" one got hit in the head. Your team is behind. You need a hit. Your team is counting on you—they are cheering your name. Your coach is telling you from the coach's box that the team needs a hit (as if you didn't know that). He says, "You can do it!" though you suspect he doesn't believe it himself. Your parents are in the stands yelling encouragement.

Three guys ahead of you have been hit, the ball making an unmistakable, sickening hollow thump like a huge dart hitting the cork before ricocheting to the screen off of rib cages and thighs and batting helmets. Sure, grownups feel fear some days, but outside of medical procedures, the expectation of sharp physical pain just doesn't come up for most of them, certainly not combined with a dreadful anticipation of failure.

Fear on the diamond isn't limited to hitters, of course. The catcher in that very situation is fearful that his pitcher will finally throw a strike and he will miss it so that the runner will score from third, or that the hitter will hit him with the bat or foul a ball off somewhere he doesn't have padding, or that the hitter will put the ball in play and the runner coming home from third will slam into him while he waits for a tardy throw. The pitcher is scared of walking in a run or getting hit by line drive. The fielders are afraid of missing an easy play. You'd think all this scary stuff would be daunting to kids. But in truth, children return to the diamond because they develop courage.

It's important to understand the duality of courage. First, a lot of the time fear is the same thing as self-doubt. Learning, and the confidence that comes with it, can help create courage by lessening fear. A batter who has been coached on the proper way to avoid an inside pitch will be more confident and less fearful. Oddly enough, a player who has been plunked a few times and found out the world doesn't end will be less fearful, too. The doubts—*can I get out of the way?* or *can I get hit and not be embarrassed by crying like a baby?*—are replaced by confidence and courage.

Fear is not limited to youth baseball. Converted catcher Scott Hatteberg was certainly not excited about his first few games as a first baseman for the A's. Major league hitters may or may not admit it, but going to the plate against Bob Gibson made at least some of them swallow hard. Getting ready to throw a fastball to Hank Aaron with the bases loaded probably gave more than one pitcher butterflies. Gaining skill and confidence will help conquer the part of fear that is self-doubt.

Second, though, is dealing with the part of fear that cannot be overcome by confidence or education. Fear of it hurting when someone hits you in the chest with a baseball is not going to be completely vanquished by knowledge that most of the time you can get out of the way. What is required is courage. Courage does not mean you aren't afraid. Courage means that you are afraid, and you do what you want to do or need to do anyway. If there was nothing to be afraid of, courage wouldn't enter the discussion. You only need courage, after all, when something scary is happening. Being courageous is a skill that can be developed by practice. Baseball gives you lots of scary situations to let you practice courage.

Learning what fear feels like and how to deal with it is a skill that you don't just need to have, you have to have it. Adults do have to get root canals, take the SAT, go to job performance reviews, and merge onto the interstate during rush hour.

Perhaps that's why hordes of otherwise overprotective parents sit their kids down to watch *The Wizard of Oz*. The child shows his or her own courage by watching the movie and observing the courage of Dorothy and company as they follow the yellow brick road, and by following the lion as he quests for courage.

The problem with learning courage this way is the limited repetition. You can only be scared of those flying monkeys once or twice, and the fact is that if things get too intense, you just remind yourself it's all make-believe, or you hide behind the sofa. There is no such option in baseball. Every youth baseball team has three or four pitchers (frequently including one who is unusually large for his age with lousy control) and you get two or three at bats a game. After living through that, making a presentation to the biggest client's CEO is as easy as playing centerfield behind Tom Seaver.

Lesson #13
Be Ready

Winning is the science of being totally prepared.

—George Allen

Occasionally you will hear ignorant people say they don't like baseball because of how "slow" or "boring" or "long" a baseball game is. I feel sorry for those folks. I mean the ones who have genuinely tried to enjoy the game but cannot because they don't understand or appreciate its inexorable rhythms.

Sure, a baseball game can take a long time to play. Players do spend time standing around. Sometimes players seem to be doing little besides staring at each other, though if you were in their minds you'd be shocked at how much there is to know and do in a game.

It is precisely this timing, this rhythm, that teaches one of baseball's best lessons—be ready. By being ready, I mean more than simply having your gear and the mental attitude to play the game at all times. Being ready is equal parts patience, self-discipline, and thinking on your feet.

One day as my wife and I waited in line at the concession stand, we struck up a conversation with a player from the younger leagues. He might have been five. He was either a little shy or rightly wary of strangers, but baseball has a way of making strangers into your friends pretty quickly. I think he decided that if our boys played baseball, we must not really be strangers.

He was the kind of kid who enjoyed the game. Grass and dirt stains showed through on his jersey and pants. His cleats were a dirty mess. It was hot and the sweat had cut clean streaks through the grime on his face. In short, he reminded me of my kids, who were by now much older and in the big diamond/steel cleat league.

After trying to get him to talk for a minute or two, my wife finally asked, "What is your favorite position?"

He thought just a second and said in two very distinct syllables, "*Hit-ter.*" It may have been the most honestly answered baseball question in the history of the game. Everyone wants to hit, and for a good player, the time between at bats can seem endless.

Nothing teaches patience like waiting your turn at bat. Kids are way more interested in where they fall in the batting order than where they'll be playing in the field (except for some pitchers, but that's a different learning of patience). Waiting while your name moves slowly up the list, batter by batter, till it is your turn to hit teaches patience in the most exacting way.

Of course, baseball teaches patience in lots of other ways, too. The best hitters are the ones patient in the count, waiting for pitches they can hit hard until two strikes, perhaps even fouling off pitches they could not hit hard in order to see one more. These hitters lay off the soft, floating, cap-bill-high pitches that they can't handle, hoping for one belt-high that crosses too much of the plate.

Relief pitchers sit patiently for endless innings in the bullpen, waiting for a starter to tire. They wait knowing that even if the starter tires, the manager may choose another reliever. A reliever may warm up three or four times in a game and never see the mound. Pinch hitters have it the worst. They sit in the dugout and watch the game, only to be called on when the game is in its most critical situation to try to deliver an important hit for their team.

There are countless other scenarios—waiting for the pitcher to take his warm-up tosses, waiting while the hitter gets himself set, waiting for a ball to be hit to you, waiting while the coach visits the mound, waiting for the next day, or next season, to come and bring redemption for shortcomings of games past. Baseball will teach you patience, if you are smart enough to let it. Being ready means that when your patience is rewarded with your turn, you are able to compete at your best.

Beyond patience, the second part of being ready is self-discipline. I try to teach that self-discipline is understanding that sometimes you have to do things you don't particularly want to do and sometimes you don't get to do things that you really do want to do. The "self" part of self-discipline means making yourself do or forgo doing something *and* feeling good about, or at least accepting the situation with grace.

Good baseball players—outside of the ones who are extraordinarily physically gifted—usually have a great deal of self-discipline. All those who play for a long time at a high level do, even the ones with special talents.

The great Cal Ripken, Jr., played in 2,632 consecutive Major League Baseball games. To do that took great skill, great endurance, and yes, a little bit of luck. Mostly what it took, though, was the self-discipline to keep himself in top shape and ready to play, day after day.

Julio Franco was born in 1958. He was still playing baseball when he was forty-eight years old. Only twenty four home runs have been hit by players older than forty-five in modern major league history. All but five of those home runs were hit by Julio Franco. His ability to still perform at the major league level is attributable to his fantastic physical condition. He worked very hard, during the season and out of it, to stay in that physical condition.

It takes self-discipline to continue to work like that—to work out on days when you'd probably rather be doing something else. It takes self-discipline to continue to push yourself to achieve when you have met most of your goals. Self-discipline is the part of being ready that makes you the master of your most consistent adversary—yourself.

Self-discipline also means willing yourself to do your job despite what is going on around you. Occasionally a game will seem so slow that a player will fall into the trap of watching the game instead of playing the game. From time to time this is not a matter of simple boredom.

A third baseman, even a very good one, can become hypnotized by a pitcher who is pitching a terrific game. If he is not careful, he may turn into a mere spectator and be watching the ball that comes sailing toward him rather than playing it. A baseball player has to have the self-discipline to know that while he is watching the game he also has to be playing the game.

The one/one pitch with no one on and one out in the bottom of the second may seem like a relatively dull point in the game, until you let the ball hop over your glove and suddenly a routine out is a runner in scoring position.

The last part of being ready is thinking on your feet. Baseball situations are constantly changing. Often, unlike a more continuous sport like soccer or basketball, there are breaks in the action to reset, recalibrate, reconsider what you are doing. In that way, baseball is more like life than many other sports. Baseball also gives you the chance to experience those rushing moments when you must adjust your plan at the last minute to compensate for current events.

For example, with two on and one out, a ball may be hit into the gap between the left fielder and the centerfielder and roll to the fence. The shortstop, previously playing up the middle and hoping for the double-play ball, must now turn and run to the cutoff spot in short left field. He has to watch the outfielders retrieve the ball, but he also must set himself so as to cut off the throw (that is, catch it and redirect it to the spot on the infield where it must go).

So while his eyes watch the fielders, his ears must listen for his teammates to tell him where to throw. He has to block out the distractions. He has to know whether his fielder has enough arm strength to get him the ball. In short, in a pressure-filled situation, he must know what to do and how to do it, and adjust to the game's changing conditions.

The same is true for the hitter who just hit one into the gap. He must control his urge to celebrate; he has to concentrate on getting to first, watching his first-base coach to see if he is being waved or told to turn and look; he must find the ball and his third-base coach with his eyes, while remembering to step on first as he goes by. If the throw comes to third or the plate, he has to gauge whether he can make it to second before the throw. If the second baseman is out of position, will he be able to make it to an uncovered bag? He must remember how many are out. If he's tagged for out three before a run crosses the plate, that run will not count. Once the ball is back on the infield, he has to hustle back to the last base he touched to keep from getting tagged out.

One season, I coached a seven-year-old named Grant in the machine pitch league. He may have been the smallest player in the league. As my wife said, he went straight from his Stride Rites to his cleats. Near the beginning of our season, as teams were still sorting themselves out, we had a late weeknight game. What had started as a chilly night had turned downright cold. Then, it started to rain.

It was the bottom of the last inning. We had already won because of the scoring rules and the other team was taking its last at bat, just as a learning exercise. The umpire headed home. The other team had one player who had not come close to hitting a ball all night. As the coach worked with her in the batter's box, positioning her hands and feet, encouraging her to keep her head still, etc., I secretly wished things would just hurry up and end.

As I looked out over my defense, some looking up at the rain, most with their heads down watching small puddles start to form at their feet, I noticed Grant, far out in left field where I had sent him. Everyone within sight of the game, including Grant, knew that the player in the batter's box had no more chance of hitting the baseball into the outfield than we did of seeing a rainbow, yet there stood Grant in the "ready" position. Chin thrust out, eyes staring at the plate, ignoring the water dripping off the bill of his cap, Grant was ready. Grant got a game ball that night, not for what he did, but for what he was.

You have to be ready, in baseball and in the rest of life. Learn patience, self-discipline, and how to think on your feet. You will never regret knowing any of these things and will always be better off for it.

Lesson #12
Take Advantage of Your Opportunities

Some say opportunity knocks only once. That is not true. Opportunity knocks all the time, but you have to be ready for it.
—Louis L'Amour

During a rain delay when the coaches, players, and fans from four different games were all seeking shelter under the same eight-by-sixteen-foot concession stand canopy, I listened to one of the most interminable baseball arguments ever, and I've heard a lot. Two of my then-colleagues were discussing the best place to "hide" their worst fielder—left field or right field.

The consensus was that centerfield was where you played your best outfielder, so as to have someone who could cover the most territory and help the other two. I don't remember how it came out. I think I went for a hot dog. The fact of the matter, though, is that most youth league coaches at the lower levels do put their weaker players in either left or right field and hope for grounders on the infield.

If you've never coached a team (and your kid has spent some time in one or the other of those spots), you would assume that's because all youth baseball coaches are hard driving, win-at-any-cost tyrants who take some players because they have to and just want them where they can do the least damage. In some cases, you'd be right.

On the other hand, you need to know that not every coach in

every league is like that. From a coach's perspective, you have other considerations. One of the prime considerations is player safety. After about three practices, you get a pretty good idea about who can get their glove up in time to, if not field a line drive, at least protect their face. It's not all about baseball skill and reaction time either. Sometimes, it's about whether the kid will remember that he has to pay attention on every single pitch.

No matter how good he is with a glove, a kid who stares off into space, talks to his friends outside the fence during the game, or is distracted every time somebody walks their dog behind the dugout has no business at third base. Sooner or later some hitter is going to hit a line drive down his throat.

For me, at least, the coaching nightmare was not losing three in a row because my third baseman couldn't catch the ball. The nightmare was seeing a kid face reconstructive dental visits because I put him in a position that he couldn't yet handle. The most important part of that sentence is, of course, *yet*. Because the player who can't handle that buzzing line drive the second practice of the season may be able to do so by, say, the third game. The challenge is to gauge that improvement.

When, as a coach, do you think that you can put young Lefty at third base instead of deep left field and not risk the team's chance to win a game, not to mention his future career as a model for toothpaste commercials? I'll tell you when. It's when the player takes advantage of the opportunities he does get.

Some players spend the entire season out in left field, figuratively and literally. There's lots of flora and fauna to deal with out there in left—four-leaf clovers, dandelions, anthills, butterflies, grasshoppers. There are also towering fly balls that are higher than the blue jays fly and hard-bouncing grounders that skitter around on the uneven turf like rabbits running from the terriers.

And what you watch for as a coach is that special day that Ol' Lefty finally puts it all together. Because one day Lefty will get an opportunity he takes advantage of. It'll probably be late in a game and the other team will have a runner on second and a good hitter at the plate. The other team's coach will be urging his hitter to hit it in the outfield to drive the run home.

The runner on second will be dying for a ball that will get out of the infield so he can round third and slide at home plate (whether he needs to or not, he'll want to slide in—they all do).

The right-handed hitter will do as asked, getting his bat around on an inside pitch and driving it hard between the third baseman and shortstop, and it'll bounce once hard and high just past the edge of the dirt. The man on second will grin and start running home, and the fans on both teams will start watching Lefty, who has seen more than his fair share of these go bouncing like a rabbit to the fence. The hitting team will quickly look out at Lefty, gauge their chances based on his prior performances, and be excited. His teammates will try not to groan aloud.

This day, though, is different. Instead of watching the bee on the clover blossom, Lefty was watching the plate. Instead of being shocked into attention by a screaming coach or parent or teammate, Lefty was in the "ready position." This time Lefty smoothly glides across the uneven outfield and instead of stumbling and maybe falling, he charges the ball and gloves it shoe-top high on an easy bounce, and he's still moving, running, all his momentum toward the plate.

For one surreal minute, everything goes quiet. On the other side, thrilled expectation has been replaced by sudden concern. On Lefty's side, it's astonishment and shock. The third-base coach stops lazily waving his arm and begins yelling for the runner to hurry.

The runner, unable to see the play now behind him, picks up on the change in emotion. The catcher, previously standing in front of the plate holding his mask just in case things went so badly that there might be a play on the hitter, throws his mask toward the backstop and, still not quite believing, settles into a half-crouch.

The pitcher has to hustle to back him up. The shortstop, who until now was running toward the outfield in case Lefty didn't notice the ball, peels off, mouth open, palms turned to the sky, and begins yelling, "Four, four, four," hoping Lefty doesn't sail it into centerfield instead. Last of all, the guilty third baseman settles into his cutoff position and stares.

Calmly and precisely Lefty takes two steps, maybe even crow hops, and lets fly at the astonished catcher, who, without believing he is saying it, screams, "Let it through!" The third baseman, who can now believe neither what he has seen nor heard, pulls his glove out of the way and backs out of the catcher's field of view. The catcher now comes ready, putting his leg across the dirt just up the third base line as the runner, now fully sensing the urgency, runs for all he is worth.

Lefty's throw bounces once and hits the mitt dead center. The startled catcher leans left, holding the ball inside his mitt with his bare hand, and tags the runner, maybe even remembering to come up to a throwing position to stop the hitter's advance. The umpire, suddenly transformed from a bored squeaky-voiced teenager to a skinny Harry Wendelstedt, lifts his left leg, spins on the ball of his right foot, makes a fist, punches it in the air at the runner, and screams in a voice loud enough to be heard even in the lonely land that is left field, "You're out!" The whole thing took about eight seconds.

For a brief moment, everything is as quiet as a church after the amen of the benediction. Then, all is bedlam. The opposing coach is letting the runner have it for not getting home on the single. The astonished coaches have recovered enough to start yelling equal parts instruction and praise; the astonished fans cheer for the effort and shout out Lefty's name.

Lefty's even more astonished parents accept the congratulations of the other parents on the team, who now profess that they knew Lefty could do it all the time. Lefty's teammates call his name and cheer. The catcher points at him before he snaps his mask back on. The pitcher taps his chest as if to say "my bad" and makes a mental note not to throw any more inside pitches to that guy. The only one who seems unaffected is Lefty, who turns and jogs back out to his position, maybe holding a finger aloft to indicate the out, as if to say, "Of course I threw him out." But Lefty is smiling inside, and so is Lefty's coach.

For reasons I wish I understood, more often than not, a single play like that has a chance to turn a kid who was a terrible player into a solid one, and a solid one into a crackerjack. A play or two or three like that, and Lefty will be taking over in a few innings for the third baseman who was tardy getting to the cutoff spot. The coach will still cringe a bit when the hard one is hit toward third. Lefty may even boot a few, but he's likely to take advantage of his opportunities again.

Not every left fielder turns into an infield star. Some of them stay out there and become outfield stars. Once in awhile, an opportunity will come along. Sometimes it's one you've prepared for over time. Sometimes, it's one you haven't prepared for, but you see an opportunity and you take it. The point is that, in either circumstance, you have to make the most of the opportunities that you get when they come along.

When the great Miller Huggins decided in June of 1925 to

bench some of the veterans who had let the Yankees slide to more than ten games out of first, he put former Columbia University star Lou Gehrig at first base (don't believe all that stuff about Wally Pip getting beaned in batting practice that day, blah, blah, blah; Huggins knew what he was doing). Gehrig took advantage of the opportunity. He wasn't the immediate shining star some of his biographies would lead you to believe, but he did well enough that day and improved over time until no one else started a game at first base for the Yankees for the next fourteen years.

Whatever you do in life, opportunities will come. They will probably even be easy to recognize. The task is to make sure that when opportunity comes bouncing across the field at you, you pick it up and rifle it home.

Lesson #11
Everyone Can Contribute

Judge not, according to the appearance.

—John 7:24

One of the best lessons of youth baseball is that no matter how good you are, you have room to improve, and no matter how bad you are, you can still contribute to the effort. Our illustrations of this lesson run from the sublime to the ridiculous, but there was hardly a season where we did not see a stark example.

In my son Rob's second year of Tee Ball, I agreed to help coach his team. I was more than a little worried about doing this. I played youth baseball growing up and watched baseball on TV, but that's all. The league gave each coach a copy of the official rules of baseball, including the rules peculiar to our park. They told us not to yell at the umpires, to collect the candy money, and to make sure the whole team was there early on picture day. That was the extent of our "training." Was that enough to teach the game? More importantly, was that enough to teach a love for the game to kids who were still learning to cut, paste, and color?

John, the head coach, had played a lot more baseball than I had and was very knowledgeable. I counted on him to cover the difficult fundamentals and intricacies of the game. I would be the cheerleader and shag balls. Maybe it would be enough.

I needn't have worried. We spent the first practice not learning about swing mechanics and base running technique but learning the names of the bases and in which direction they were run. When the time came for mechanical instruction, real baseball, I was able to rely on John's knowledge, while I was more hands-on—literally.

One child, Mike, was almost sad to watch. His first attempt at throwing a baseball ended up with him falling, quite literally, on his face. He lined up sideways to his target and somehow tried to move his back leg in front of his front leg while twisting his body and whipping his arm around about waist high. He hit the ground hard, face first. Worse, he never let go of the ball.

Even the other five-year-olds began to groan. I spent part of an interminable spring afternoon working with Mike. That day I literally held his feet and moved them while Coach John moved his arms. I didn't know if Mike would come back to the next practice. I was scared for Coach John to hit him a ball in infield practice.

But Mike came back and kept coming back. By the end of the season, he played regularly on the infield. In one game he had three put-outs, fielding the ball and throwing it to first. On the day he got the "game ball" and listened to the cheers of his teammates and parents, his smile was worth twice the hours I put into the whole season.

In the first game of the 1988 World Series, the Los Angeles Dodgers' best offensive threat was sitting in the clubhouse watching the game on TV. Kirk Gibson had two injured legs and was on the roster but not expected to play the entire series. He could contribute through his wisdom, experience, and leadership but not on the field of play. He could hardly walk without hobbling, much less run the ninety feet between the bases. Nonetheless, near the end of game one with the Dodgers behind by a run, Gibson began to warm up in the clubhouse. With two outs and one on in the ninth, Gibson "walked" to the plate to pinch hit against future Hall of Fame pitcher Dennis Eckersly.

Watching his first swing, even on videotape, is as painful as any sight in baseball, next to seeing the heroic Dave Dravecky break his cancer-weakened pitching arm during his comeback bid in 1989. In case you are one of the ten living Americans who does not know, Gibson hit the game-winning home run. His journey around the bases makes you wonder how he climbed the dugout steps without help. His home-run blast ignited the Dodgers, and although he did not play again in the series, the Dodgers beat the heavily favored A's.

Never, ever judge anyone on their physical appearance. In the first place, judging other people based on how they look is unfair and disrespectful. (That's enough, in and of itself, to end the discussion.)

In the second place, judging people based on their appearance violates the Golden Rule—everyone wants to be judged on their own talent, spirit, ability, and effort, not their skin color, height, weight, or whether they have curly hair. Don't assume someone is a lousy baseball player because they wear glasses, and they won't assume you are a lousy baseball player because you are skinny.

In the third place, judging people based on their appearance will make you wrong more times than you are right. So if you can't remember this lesson because it is the proper thing to do, or because of the Golden Rule, then try to remember it so you don't look stupid.

Baseball will teach you this lesson pretty quickly. In fact, one reason I like baseball so much is that it's the last sport I know of that is not dominated at the professional level by physical freaks of nature. You can spot a pro football lineman in the mall from half a mile away. He's the size of a stand-alone ATM. Most of the time, you wouldn't know that the average professional second baseman is a professional athlete if you were standing behind him in line at the food court.

I've seen and coached fat kids who could run and skinny kids whom you could time to first base with a calendar. I've seen tall kids who couldn't catch and short kids who could hit it to the fence. Baseball allows, in some cases even requires, different physical types to do different things. Let people show you what they can do and evaluate them on their ability, talent, spirit, and work. If you do, you can expect that in return from them.

Everyone can contribute something. Whether you are an incredibly talented star like Kirk Gibson who hits a dramatic homer when some people said you didn't belong on the World Series roster, or a kid who learns to field and throw a baseball to a target dependably, or just someone's dad whose job is to hold small arms and legs and show them how to work, everyone has something to offer. If they are willing to try and you are willing to give them a chance, everyone will win.

You need to find out, in every situation that matters, what you have to offer and what those around you can offer, too. Failing to make that effort yourself and to give others a chance to show what they can do is not only going to deprive you of opportunities, it is wrong. Don't do it.

Lesson #10
Practice Does Not Make Perfect, But . . .

Practice is the best of all instructors.

—Publius Syrus

Practice is fun for a couple of times in the first year of youth baseball. Some coaches make it more fun than others. In fact, there's at least one entire book out there about how to make baseball practice more fun. Even many of the youngest and most enthusiastic players hate to practice. By nature and definition, it is repetitive and time-consuming. In fact, practice is like a lot of jobs. But even young players quickly come to distinguish and respect the individual kids who practice at home and the teams whose coaches make their practice productive.

Publius Syrus understood it fifty years before Christ was born and he probably did not invent the idea. Even five-year-olds who do not grasp many abstract concepts (and most don't) understand that the more times they swing and hit the ball off the tee in the backyard, the fewer times they will miss and the farther the ball will fly.

The trick is to get them to internalize the lesson that what works in Tee Ball also works in life. The best magicians, brain surgeons, poets, trial lawyers, sales agents, carpenters, and truck drivers are the ones who spend time diligently improving themselves and the practice of their craft.

U.S. News and World Report recently went to great lengths to demonstrate that hospitals that are most successful at particular procedures were invariably the ones who had professionals who had performed the procedures many times. I suppose they needed the data to back it up, but any kid who has ever taken batting practice could have told them that would be the case.

The bad news is that practice almost never makes you "perfect." Most things worth doing involve practice, and perfect is an unattainable goal. The good news is that after admitting that, practice bridges the deep gap between where you started out and just this side of perfect. Practice nearly always makes you better and is usually the difference between fair and good, as well as good and excellent. Beyond that, practice instills confidence and a sense of accomplishment, just as surely as Albert Pujols pounds hanging curve balls over the fence.

In youth baseball, the better teams tend to practice more, or get more out of their practices, than the other teams. Some teams do have one or two terrific players with God-given ability, but rarely do one or two players win the game by themselves. The ability of the other players is necessary. The difference for those other players is practice.

Somewhere buried in the practice concept is a word I try not to use around young players. Practice is work. Baseball is a game. For the majority of the world, baseball is a children's pastime. It is a game to be enjoyed and played, not worked at. Practice, though—whether it's baseball, cursive writing, or computer programming—is work. I just try not to say it out loud. Instead, I often tell them that Ted Williams, arguably the greatest hitter ever, said, "The harder I work, the luckier I seem to get."

Knowing that you need to practice, and knowing how, is work and a valuable life lesson. What applies to fielding, pitching, and hitting applies equally to playing the violin, reading x-rays, and cooking pancakes. By practicing, you get better and know you are better.

Lesson #9
There's No Substitute for God-Given Ability

What we are is God's gift to us. What we become is our gift to God.
—Eleanor Powell

Here's another painful and disappointing addition to the list—at least for most people. It is a simple fact that if you live very long you will find people, sometimes a great number of people, who can do things you do and do them better. God, for very good reasons of His own, just did not make us all precisely the same.

Sometimes you can overcome a perceived deficit with practice, concentration, and perseverance. Sometimes, however, all the practice, attention to detail, and concentration in the world will not make you as talented as someone who just has sheer God-given ability.

The shocking truth is that sometimes talented people hardly even seem to try. Some kids never learn to hit a curve ball—actually, quite a lot of them never do. Some kids, through repetition and concentration, can learn to recognize and hit that peculiar pitch. A few kids can and do hit it and, well, those kids never seem to think two things about it.

If you don't believe that God makes us all, you can call it genetics, or evolution, or talent, or whatever you will. But the simple fact is that there are players who just naturally seem to recognize and understand what the ball does as it reaches the plate, and they will dependably smack curve balls out of the infield as long as the pitcher will throw them.

Likewise, some players are naturally gifted outfielders and from the crack of the bat have an exceptional understanding of where the ball will go and how quickly it will get there. Over time a player can learn these skills, but they will simply never be quite as good as the player who has that little extra something called God-given ability.

Our friend Aaron was a good hitter and fielder and a good kid. Through most of youth baseball he had played on the infield and liked it. When he moved up to the big diamond (a stage where lots of kids hang up their spikes), Aaron found out there were lots of good hitters and infielders around.

At a cold, gray, early spring practice, as everyone's eyes watered from the cold wind, Coach Randy said, "Fellows, we've got lots of infielders on this team. I'm looking for a centerfielder to anchor my outfield. Has anyone played much centerfield?" No hands went up. "Well," the coach continued, "anyone want to give it a try?" Budding young shortstops and first basemen stared at the grass. Outfield had always been where the questionable players went to hide.

Finally, Aaron raised his hand. "I'll try it, Coach." Within a couple of practices, everyone knew that Aaron was now playing where he always should have. On fly balls he seemed to know instinctively at the crack of the bat how far the ball would fly. Without being told, on a long hit he would immediately turn his back on the infield and run to where the ball was headed. He covered lots of ground in a hurry. He could make a diving catch and keep his elbow off the turf so the ball didn't jar out of his glove. Things that a young player needed to be coached to do, Aaron did automatically.

By the middle of that season, he looked like a Tee Ball player if the team took infield grounders, but in the outfield, he set the standard. Routine fly balls turned into routine outs. Line drives in the gap were cut off before rolling to the fence. Balls with ambitions of being doubles or triples became just noisy singles.

Middle infielders now ran to cutoff positions, knowing they might be doing some good. Aaron made it to the All-Stars in centerfield that season and all the succeeding seasons we watched him play. He was a natural at centerfield. It wasn't anything anyone taught him, and it couldn't totally be explained by the hours and hours of repetition, either.

This lesson will hold true in all walks of life. Some people sit down and play the piano with little struggle or seeming effort. Others take lessons for years and never learn to play music, as opposed to just pressing the keys. Some people can draw, some can make speeches, and some can juggle bowling balls. As hard as we try, we can approach the skills of these individuals, but it will never be as easy for us as it is for them.

Just learn to get used to it. The trick of this lesson is to learn how to appreciate and admire the special gifts and skills of talented people without letting jealousy consume you. Don't give up trying to achieve their levels just because they do it more easily than you.

Become comfortable with the fact that there's almost always someone who can perform a particular feat more quickly, easily, or gracefully than you do. You don't have to be complacent about it and should never give up trying to achieve their level, but don't lose sight of the fact that we are not, after all, created exactly equal. The good news is that you probably do something—maybe more than one thing—more easily and naturally than other people do. Find the talents that you have and maximize those. Nothing more is necessary; nothing less is required.

Lesson #8
Winning Is Important

For when the One Great Scorer comes
To write against your name,
He marks—not that you won or lost—
But how you played the game.

—Grantland Rice

I expect that the great sportswriter Grantland Rice spins around in his grave like a Nolan Ryan fastball every time some well-intentioned adult takes some version of the last two lines of his poem "Alumnus Football" and perverts it into "it's just fine and dandy to lose." I don't think that's what Rice meant, and not by a long way.

If Rice genuinely thought that winning didn't matter, do you think the Football Writers Association of America would have named its college football trophy, given annually to the NCAA Division I champion, after him? Would he have written the famous poem "Casey's Revenge" if he thought it was just fine for the Mighty Casey of Mudville to be remembered for one bad at bat in a losing effort? I think not.

Rice's point is well taken and, read in context, is a genuinely important truth. Yes, I suspect that God Almighty does not much keep up with victories and losses in the scoreboard sense of things. He is, I believe, much more concerned about things like duty, sportsmanship, and loving thy neighbor.

I have watched too much youth league baseball not to believe that He also intervenes to keep players—not to mention younger siblings, spectators, and even hard-hearted coaches sitting on sunflower-seed buckets in the dugout door—safe. If, before speaking or acting, everyone stopped to think "how does this affect my character in the perspective of eternity?," almost everything in the world would be better.

However, if the best thing you can think of to tell a child who has just lost (whether at baseball or tiddlywinks or whatever) is, "Don't worry about it kid, 'cause when you are dead and get to heaven God isn't going to care that you lost today," well, better just pat them on the back and don't say anything. You are not making them feel any better.

I suppose for the sake of argument it would be nice to live in a Utopian sort of society where winning and losing counted not a fig. I suppose. But the harsh truth is that this isn't Utopia, and winning does matter.

Similarly, the idea that "you can't win them all" doesn't mean that you shouldn't try or that you shouldn't be bothered when you do lose. Winning matters and I want my kids to know it. As I intend to teach the lesson, winning does not necessarily mean always beating the other competitor or the other team. Scoring as high as you possibly can on the math test is winning in my book. Being on a team that loses 5-4 on a day when you went 2 for 3 with an RBI and scored a run can be a winning day for you. Some days, just getting a ball into play against a pitcher who has owned you for the entire season may be a win.

My point is that victories, large and small, count. It is important to win, and it is important not to think it is OK to lose because it will all even out in heaven or because you have to lose some of them.

Think about it. When was the last time the president of the

United States called up the losing team in the locker room and told them that losing was OK?

Our society keeps score, in baseball, in the stock market, or in total number of boxes of Girl Scout cookies sold. Baseball teaches that winning is important. How to handle winning and losing is important, but the simple primary concept that winning is important cannot and should not be avoided—poetry and well-meaning adults aside.

Lesson #7
Don't Give Up

It ain't over till it's over.

—Yogi Berra

Youth baseball may be the best place in all the world to test Yogi Berra's improperly maligned statement that "it ain't over till it's over." Youth baseball games that are still mathematically within reach of the team that is behind are always at risk. Games that are no longer at risk are declared complete by the umpire and everyone gets to have a snack and go home.

So as long as the game is on, you are within reach of winning. It is not unheard of for six runs to walk in without a single hit, even with two out in the last inning. I know—I have sat through it. The idea, like Berra's, extends beyond the actual games themselves, too.

Young baseball players at the lowest levels regularly reach first base on weak bouncing balls to the infielders. Just because you barely hit it is no reason not to run as hard as you can. The ball might hit a rock and bounce wildly toward the dugout, it might roll right between someone's legs, it might be fielded cleanly and so startle the fielder that they forget to throw it to first, it might be thrown and sail not only over the first baseman's head but over the fence and across the sidewalk, or it might go whizzing into the first baseman's mitt as if shot from a cannon, just ahead of you, but the umpire looked down at his buzzing cell phone at the same instant and missed both calls.

I read once that there are over twenty ways for a Major League Baseball player to reach first base within the rules. I'll bet there are about two hundred ways that a player can reach first base safely in youth baseball, but only if the hitter does not give up. It also works in reverse. Just because a player hits a ball and you don't field it cleanly does not mean you should give up.

The hitter might forget to run, fall down, or run toward third base instead of first (seen this). The hitter might decide that it is more important at that moment to visit the restroom than the other end of the first base line (didn't see this but heard about it). Even if the ball goes under your glove, through your legs, and you have to chase it, don't give up, because you never can tell what might happen.

In 2004, the Boston Red Sox were in more trouble than a squirrel trying to cross Boylston Street at rush hour. The Red Sox were down three games to none to the mighty New York Yankees in the American League Championship series. They had lost the first three games of the series by a combined score of 32-15, including an embarrassing 19-8 shellacking the night before in a game that was, quite honestly, not as close as the final score indicated. The Red Sox had to beat the Yankees to even stay alive, much less think about going to the World Series.

In addition, the Red Sox had a painful and well-documented history of losses that hung around their collective neck like a bat weight on a Louisville Slugger. Boston had not won a World Series since 1919. In some of those years, there were heartrending losses for Red Sox fans (for what it's worth, I don't think Buckner beats Wilson to the bag in '86, even if Knight wouldn't have scored from second on the infield hit, although I'll admit his going 0-5 was not helpful—but I digress) and even more seasons where they were just downright lousy.

When the great Yankee player Alex Rodriguez hit a two-run homer in the third that not only went over the vaunted Green Monster in left but sailed completely out of Fenway Park, Boston did not give up. Neither did their fans. Red Sox supporters outside the stadium caught the ball and threw it back into the park, twice. Boston rallied (with two outs) for three runs in the fifth inning to take a 3-2 lead. It was only their second lead of the series, and the first had lasted exactly one-half inning.

The Yankees took the lead back again, scoring two runs in the next half-inning. Boston didn't give up. The nearly unhittable Yankee relief pitcher Mariano Rivera took a one-run lead to the mound in the ninth inning, with a chance to close it out for the Yankees. Rivera had already saved two games in the series and the Red Sox had not scored on him, but Boston would not give up. The Red Sox squeezed out a run to tie the game.

Eventually, Boston won 6-4 in twelve innings. The next night, Boston trailed 4-2 going to the bottom of the eighth inning, but they did not give up, and they won again in fourteen innings. They eventually won the World Series in one of the most improbable comebacks in baseball history. It would have been easy for the Red Sox to give up in game four, but they didn't. They now all have World Series rings, and their fans have memories that will last a lifetime, simply because they persevered.

As young players get older and more sophisticated, they tend to commit fewer errors and turn grounders on the infield into routine outs, but this is not always so. Hits that clear the infield usually result in the batter reaching first safely, but not always. Usually teams with large leads hold them in the ninth inning, but not always.

Even at the major league level, every player who hits the ball runs all the way to first base and touches it—even if they know, absolutely, that they are out and the fielding team has already thrown it back to the pitcher. There's always the chance that something might happen during the routine play. Even a team that is way behind in the ninth inning does not just pack up its bats and cleats and walk back up the tunnel. While you still have three outs, or even one, you still have a chance.

Most of the time, things work out the way you expect. Plays and games that look as though they are over generally are. But you still have to persevere, because you never know. A lot of successful people will tell you that they failed lots of times but that they just kept trying until they succeeded. This can-do, sometimes-you-get-away-with-one spirit applies to almost every undertaking in life.

Most of the time, another guy gets the big promotion. Usually the lady down the row hits the progressive slot machine jackpot in Las Vegas. The prettiest girls go to the dance with someone more handsome or more popular or more witty than you. But if you keep on trying, someday, sometime, you'll get the big promotion, you'll hit the jackpot, and the prettiest girl will say yes to you—and then some other guy will be jealous and it will be his turn to keep on trying.

Even if you're down by five in the bottom of the sixth (we don't play nine innings in youth leagues), stand in, hold the bat back, and keep your eye on the ball. Because if you don't give up, eventually you will succeed.

Lesson #6
Some Rules Have Reasons

Baseball is almost the only orderly thing in a very unorderly world. If you get three strikes, even the best lawyer in the world can't get you off.
—Bill Veeck

Most kids, mine included, go through at least one phase where they question everything. I know a school principal who says this phase begins right after they learn to talk in sentences, continues for about eighteen years, and then gradually fades for the next twelve.

I know what my principal friend means, but I'm not talking about the teenage rebelliousness that declares everything boring, stupid, or worse. I mean the exciting and tremendously aggravating phase when kids have questions about everything. I've decided it is not rebellion but innate curiosity that makes them want to know the reason "why" for most everything. This includes questioning "the rules."

I happen to be one of those dads who tried to explain as much and as often as I could. Partly, I thought this was best for the boys. Partly, I found it important to occasionally reexamine what I just accepted as given. Partly, there was the challenge of seeing if they could discern when I didn't know the reason and was just making it up. (Hear the wisdom of my wife: "Oh, for heaven's sake, honey, if you don't know just tell them that.")

I did think making it up was better than giving no reason at all. ("Dad, why is there a rule that we don't sing at the table? You say people sing when they are happy and I'm happy Mom made pork loin.") "Because I'm the dad and I say so" occasionally got the silence I was after, but frankly it left me feeling as if I had failed just a little bit. It's a lame answer, and kids know it.

Baseball came to the rescue. I finally arrived at the simple answer that some rules really don't have reasons, and while those rules may be worth examining, you still have to play by the rules till they are changed. That said, "wear a batting helmet at the plate" or "wear a cup when you catch" are not rules that ever have to be explained at any level of baseball. Five minutes of watching their teammates throw inspires most youth leaguers to inquire about additional protective equipment.

Even a relatively difficult rule such as the "infield fly" rule can be made clear through a couple of examples. That is, as a fielder, you shouldn't be able to get two outs by playing badly, if playing perfectly would have only gotten one out.

However, baseball has a plateful of rules with no meaning or reasoning other than "I'm the umpire and I say so." "Dad, why is it four balls for a walk but only three strikes for an out?" Or "why can you tag up on a caught foul ball when the batter didn't succeed in hitting it fair?" There is no obvious reason for these rules. These are just the rules and you might as well get used to them.

The same explanation holds for sometimes silly rules to which we all adhere, without really having a reason. They just are. At a four-way stop, why does the car on the right get to go first? Why don't you wear dark socks with short pants? Why don't you talk to other people during elevator rides? These are just life's little rules. Learn to live with them.

The baseball analogy has served me well. The boys haven't stopped their healthy and occasionally useful questioning of authority, but they are getting used to the idea that sometimes you need a rule. Even though it may not be clear why you need it, it must be followed till there is a better rule.

Lesson #5
Play Fair

Fair play is a jewel.

—Abraham Lincoln

Play fair. Always. Do not tolerate those who do not. Because that is what is right.

Lesson #4
Working on a Team

People who work together will win, whether it be against complex football defenses or the problems of modern society.
—Vince Lombardi

One of the more obvious lessons that baseball teaches is how to work on a team. Despite what some will tell you, being good at teamwork is not an innate talent for most people. Many of our natural instincts make us really lousy team players.

Normal tendencies to make excuses for yourself, to blame others, to want all the credit for a victory and take no blame for a loss, and to think of yourself first are directly opposed to what makes a good team player.

This lesson from baseball rates high on the list because it is one of the most useful lessons that you will apply most often in life experiences. In business, the military, government, volunteer efforts, and other endeavors, the ability to function on a team and to understand the dynamics of why and how good teams do well (and poor teams fail) is critical.

By "understand" I do not mean that you have to actually be able to list and explain all the key factors of team success. I just mean that you will understand the unwritten rules of what a good team does and how it does it. You might not think about it, but you understand these rules now. It's like driving to a favorite vacation destination—you might not be able to list all the road names, turns, and distances, but driving there is easy because you have done it before.

Sometimes the thing you learn is that the team is just not very good. We saw an old teammate, Chad, at the ballpark one Saturday morning. Chad was a talented shortstop and a good contact hitter. The summer before, he had been on a championship team with our boys. They had moved up a league and Chad was now on the Padres.

"How are the Padres?" we asked.

"Oh," Chad said, "we suck. Really bad. We may not win two games this year." (The Padres won more than two games. Otherwise, Chad's assessment was pretty much on target.) With that, he shouldered his bat bag, gave a wave, and walked into the dugout to say good morning to his teammates.

It was a good lesson. Even outside of baseball, when the team is lousy, it's still your team and you have to make the best of it. You also need to recognize when a team is bad enough for you to consider moving to a different team.

I will leave it to the business professors and authors of business books to try to list all of these factors and how they apply. Here are a few of the lessons it is important to learn on the diamond about how teams function.

1. Learn to depend on others. This may be the hardest part of this lesson. Self-reliance is a great thing. Some people in the world are able to get by using only their own efforts and strengths. Those people are darn few and far between and lead, I think, a rather hardscrabble existence. For most people, however, it is necessary to work with others. Baseball teaches that you can't always do everything yourself. Once in a great while a pitcher will pitch the so-called perfect game—no hits, no errors, no walks. It's not really a perfect game. The pitcher will not strike out every hitter. The pitcher wouldn't be able to get anyone out without a catcher to field the third strike. It's a common (and truthful) saying that for a pitcher to pitch a no-hitter or a perfect game, he will have to have some outstanding defensive plays behind him. Occasionally a batter will hit a home run and score all by himself. Sometimes truly gifted and audacious players like Ty Cobb would get a hit, then steal second, third, and home. Ty Cobb was one in a century. More commonly, a batter who becomes a runner requires the efforts of others to get him home. Learning to depend on others in order to accomplish a shared goal, instead of depending completely on yourself, is a big part of teamwork.

2. Learn to be dependable. This may be almost as hard to learn as depending on others. The greatest diving stop with a hard throw from the knees at shortstop is useless if the first baseman cannot catch the ball. I cannot imagine anything in the world that helps you learn to be dependable like baseball. When the shortstop makes a great effort to catch a hit, the first baseman is waiting to catch his throw. He wants to be dependable. Why? It's not to make himself look good but to help his team. That's the lesson to learn. The same concept applies to catching fly balls, hitting with runners in scoring position, throwing strikes when your team gives you a big lead, sacrificing, getting on base late in the game with your team behind, etc. Baseball will teach you to be dependable, whether you know it or not. Youth baseball also gives the players a chance to fail in a forgiving context. Sure, some kids goof off, make physical errors, lose concentration, and let their teammates down. Baseball lets them find out what that feels like and why it is important not to do that. It makes life easier for the middle manager, drill instructor, or volunteer coordinator to work with people if they all understand this facet of teamwork and don't have to be taught it.

3. Learn to fix the problem—not affix the blame. Mistakes happen a lot in youth baseball. Some leagues are even officially called "learning leagues." As such, there are mistakes in almost endless varieties. There are those you expect—missing ground balls, throwing to the wrong base, and dropping fly balls—as well as the more egregious errors that become the stuff of legends—running the bases in the wrong direction or a base runner fielding a batted ball. Continually yelling at kids to do things they don't know how to do or can't do does no good at all. You can yell "settle under the ball" to Johnny the centerfielder until you look like Earl Weaver, but until you teach him to do it and give him the confidence that he can, you might as well be yelling at the bat rack. Kids will figure out how to fix a problem, whether it is theirs or someone else's. It's a good lesson for life. There's no use yelling at the guy who can't use the floor buffer until he gets some instruction about running it, or until you find out he can't learn it and find something else for him to do.

4. Present a united front. Being part of a team means closing ranks. You may snip and snipe at your teammates, but *nobody* else is allowed to. This is a key element of being part of a team. You belong and others don't. This doesn't always work perfectly in youth baseball, of course, but from the local five- to six-year-old team to the Navy SEALS, the old Three Musketeer ideal of all for one and one for all applies to all teams. The better ones usually are the ones who have the most cohesive front. They are certainly the happier ones, and that counts for a lot.

5. Subordinate your own interests to those of the team. Baseball, alone among the major sports, recognizes when a player subordinates his own interests to those of his team. "Sacrifice" is not a word a lot of kids hear often. That doesn't keep it from being a good word and a good concept to learn. You don't have to sacrifice all the time. Sometimes others will sacrifice for you. Youth baseball players understand early on that sometimes you have to bunt the runner over to second base, or you have to try to hit a fly ball that will allow a runner to tag up. Teams in other areas of life understand this, too. In basketball, you sometimes have to get the defense to collapse around you so your teammate gets the glory of an easy dunk (and a good teammate will acknowledge the contribution). A lawyer sometimes takes on a case that he does not want so his colleague can take a case she otherwise wouldn't have time to take. Think about how often you hear the phrase "take one for team." Some people don't like sports analogies, but that one fits. People who say it, whether they know it or not, took it from baseball.

6. Agree upon the goal. Enterprises fail every day in this country because not everyone in the business is working to achieve the same goal. If you are the only one trying to achieve a particular goal, then you don't need to be on a team. A baseball team has to have two primary goals—scoring runs for itself, and stopping the other team from scoring runs by recording outs. It's a complex game and many individuals are doing many different things, but in one way or another players have to focus on one or both of those goals. Teammates (in baseball or otherwise) who are interested only in their own personal achievements, without regard to how they fit with the team goals, become a problem. You can learn from baseball how to avoid being that problem player.

7. Follow the rules. Previous chapters in this book talk about rules. You have to follow the rules for your team and for yourself. Following the rules doesn't just mean running the bases in the right direction. It also means not getting thrown out for arguing with umpires, not trying to injure other players, and staying away from drugs and steroids. You follow the rules because it is the right thing to do. Failing to follow the rules not only hurts you, it makes you a bad teammate.

8. Have a leader or leaders you trust. Leadership is an incredibly overworked concept. We spend so much time thinking about it, talking about it, writing books about it, and attending seminars about it that I wonder sometimes when the real leaders find time to actually lead. I expect they mostly don't read those books or go to those seminars. That said, good leadership is critical to the smooth and successful operation of a team. Good leaders do lots of things and in lots of different styles, but one of the things they all have in common is they have the trust of those they lead. Baseball teaches trust in leadership and (sadly) can demonstrate quickly what happens when the leadership is not trustworthy.

9. Sometimes, you need to pick up your teammate. The concept of helping your teammate is what most people have in mind when they talk about the importance of teamwork. Arguably, it may be the most important lesson of the team concept. This is especially true when your teammate makes a mistake or fails at something. The shortstop may have made a great diving stop in the hole on a hard-hit grounder, but without a good stretch toward the outfield by the first baseman, the throw sails wide and the runner is on second. In that case, the shortstop would have been better served to stand still and watch the ball bounce into the outfield. Occasionally, the hitter ahead of you strikes out with the go-ahead run on third, and it's up to you to bring the runner home.

Life is the same, in matters great and small. It may be that the other astronaut couldn't finish attaching the solar panel to the space station and now it's up to you. Or it may just be that your spouse forgot to pick up the dry cleaning and you need it before work on Monday. In either case, good teammates help each other and cover their teammate's errors and shortfalls.

10. Don't spend all your time relying on someone else. The complementary rule to picking up your teammate is that you can't stand around all day waiting for someone else to get the job done. Sure, Lou Gehrig came up to bat in key situations many times when he knew the great Babe Ruth was standing in the on-deck circle. The reason that Gehrig was the team captain, though, was that he didn't count on the Babe to come through for him. The shortstop who catches the hard ground ball can't count on the first baseman to make an acrobatic catch every time—he needs to make the best throw he possibly can every time. Just because you are on a team, you don't get a pass on doing your best.

The best thing, though, about being on a team is learning the thrill and acceptance of being with your teammates. You don't have to be best friends with everyone on your team. In fact, you don't even have to like them all. You do have to respect them, adjust yourself to their talents when necessary, and work with them. These are valuable lessons for life. In addition, it is hard to describe or duplicate the feeling that being part of a team, especially a successful team, can provide.

As I said at the beginning of this book, there are all sorts of ways to learn these lessons. Baseball, with its careful balance of teamwork and individual performance, emphasizes the lessons that teamwork teaches. Baseball isn't the only way to learn this, but it's a darn good one.

Lesson #3
How to Lose

I hate to lose worse than anyone, but if you never lose you won't know how to act. If you lose with humility, then you can come back.
—Paul "Bear" Bryant

My younger son played on a youth league team that broke out of the gate one season a cool 0-12. In a sixteen-game season, that is a grind. All the platitudes from all the sports figures who ever lived, all the encouragement from coaches and parents, and all the postgame snacks in the world are not going to make that feel better. However, if there is one thing baseball is guaranteed to teach, it is how to lose.

Once in awhile, a youth league team will go undefeated. Such a rare occurrence is usually caused more by shenanigans in team selection than other factors. The higher up the ladder you get, the more losses you take. A professional major or minor league team that lost "only" 25 percent (forty or so) of its games in a season would be a team for the ages. Think about that for a minute. An extraordinary major league team loses more than forty times in a single year—more than once a week. A playoff team will lose fifty or sixty times in a season.

All the platitudes you would expect about losing are relevant. The "be a good sport and shake hands with the other team" drivel that everyone talks about and learns somewhere along the way, either by experience or imitation—or by having someone who is not such a good winner knock the you-know-what out of you for being a sore loser—is important.

In life and in baseball, it is imperative that you understand how to deal with adversity. Being mature and clear-headed enough to congratulate those who have bested you is foremost in learning this lesson.

To put it simply, I want my kids to learn to lose with dignity. The "be a good loser" lesson goes much deeper and influences much more than just the "good sport" part of the equation. Losing teaches us many things, including some that get a separate heading on my list, such as patience, humility, resilience, and self-criticism.

As noted previously, baseball takes lots of patience. I am not one of those people who believes that a one-strike, two-ball pitch with one on and one out in the sixth inning is a boring, meaningless pitch. It may be the very heart of the game. If that pitch is a strike, the hitter becomes defensive and much less likely to help the runner. He's also more likely to hit into a double play. If it is a ball, the pitcher must be careful and not walk the hitter, thereby creating a much better scoring opportunity for the other team, and he may throw the ball over the center of the plate and get it hammered. The runner may also decide to try and steal a base. In truth, however, there is a lot of waiting around in a baseball game.

Waiting between games can seem even longer. Waiting around after a loss seems to last forever, especially for good players on good teams. Losing will teach you to be patient (whether that is a lesson you want to learn or not). You have to be patient not only waiting for the next game but also waiting for opportunities to do well in that game.

If you make two uncharacteristic strikeouts on Saturday, and you don't get to play again until Thursday, it takes a lot of patience not to get to the plate and swing at the first pitch, as though you are John Kruk trying to hit it back to whatever country the ball was manufactured in. Like it or not, baseball will teach patience, and no part of baseball will teach patience like losing. And if you play often, you will certainly lose.

We seem to spend a lot of time worrying about our children's self-esteem. We wrongly think, I believe, that self-esteem is something that is given to you. Actually, self-esteem is something that you earn for yourself. Telling someone they are smart, talented, graceful, etc., probably doesn't hurt, but if you are making it up, kids will see through it in about two minutes. The child has to earn some of those achievements, or all this ego building is a waste of time.

At the same time that you devote time and energy to being proud of your achievements, and therefore yourself, you need to learn some humility. In this context, losing doesn't just mean losing games or championships. Very good teams lose 30 percent of the time; the best hitters fail 66 percent of the time; very good fielders see the occasional lazy fly ball glance off their glove and hit the ground.

Your team may score fifteen runs and win by the mercy rule, but you may have struck out three times to a pitcher who cringed every time he threw you a strike. You may be the fastest kid in the league but get caught stealing by a catcher whose gear is so big he looks as if he's playing dress-up in Daddy's clothes. Baseball will teach the humility that comes with losing. Once you have learned that humility, your accomplishments will seem even brighter. That's the way to build self-esteem that will last.

Losing also teaches resilience. Just as in baseball, in life you are guaranteed to lose a few. What kind of person you become hinges less on your losses than how you reacted to those losses. The most important thing to do after a loss is to pick yourself up and get back in the game.

Losing teaches you how to do this. Whether you lost the game or just dropped an easy fly ball, you have to be willing to take a deep breath and stick your nose back in there. If you can't learn this lesson about life and losing, you are in for a sorry, miserable life.

All the other lessons in this book, even the lessons about losing, will be no good to you at all if you cannot learn to "pick yourself up, dust yourself off, and start all over again." We sing that song to kids, we read the story of the little engine that could, and then we don't carefully teach the lessons that real losing brings.

The reason that dad-gum train was worried about climbing the hill in the first place had to have been that it had met a hill it couldn't climb in the past. Sure you lose some. Sure it stinks. It's what you do after you endure losing that marks the measure of your character.

Watch the end of a big baseball game sometime, especially in the playoffs. After it is over, they'll show the losing team's dugout. Nobody will be in there laughing or admiring the fireworks. You will see a few guys sitting and staring at the field, watching the other team celebrate, knowing it could have been them.

Look at the photograph of the Giants jumping around after Bobby Thomson crossed the plate—Jackie Robinson is in the foreground, hands on hips, watching. I think those players started right then to think about how to rebound so that next time they'd be the ones out there jumping up and down like fools. Good for them!

After you've learned that a loss or failure is not the end of the world and that you have to have the resilience to start over, you must be honest enough with yourself to analyze how and why you failed and what you can do to be better next time. In baseball, they talk a lot about "adjusting." When a pitcher finds a way to get you out, can you adjust so that next time he tries the same method, you put it back in his face? When a hitter smashes your curve ball, you need to adjust your pitch sequence or placement next time you pitch to him.

Make no mistake, I believe it is very, very hard to honestly analyze your own performance and decide what needs to be changed. It is harder still to admit that no amount of adjustment may help you achieve a particular goal. Most boys who have played baseball dream of playing in the big leagues. Statistically speaking, the odds of getting there are worse than the odds of lightning striking them.

So, at some point, a fatal and painful day arrives when the self-criticism is no longer "how can I hit this pitcher," but instead becomes "there is no amount of adjustment that will let me play baseball at the next level; I must adjust my dream to do something else." However, if you can learn honest self-critique early in life, you will have the key tool that will someday help you to be a successful insurance salesman, orthodontist, or restaurant manager.

Lesson #2
How to Win

When you win, you eat better, you sleep better, your beer tastes better, and your wife looks like Gina Lollabrigida.

—Johnny Pesky

Baseball teaches all aspects of winning. It teaches you how to win, the importance of winning, and the good feelings associated with striving and coming out on top. Oddly, this is one of the very reasons youth baseball is occasionally criticized.

Apparently, there are those individuals out there who think the delicate egos of the young competitors will be permanently and horribly scarred if they are forced to confront the idea of winning and losing. Well, I have bad news for them. That's precisely what I wanted my kids to confront in baseball and in life.

To an extent, though, I agree that our society puts an awful lot of emphasis on winning and losing. I tend to agree that for some kids the physical activity, the joy of playing, and the need to learn the rules should trump a focus on victory. The league my kids played in does not keep score at the very lowest level. Three outs do not make an inning, either.

However, the reason for that rule is that the concept of victory and the concept of learning to play and enjoy every game can be inimical. The concern is not about bruising egos that some apparently believe are more tender than a peeled banana. Once you've learned to play the game, you keep score.

Somebody wins and somebody loses. Like it or not, that's the way of life.

Learning how to win is a two-part lesson. The first part is learning what it takes to win. The second part is understanding how to act and react when you achieve a victory.

Winning is a habit. Teams that win on a consistent basis expect to win and have a way of making those expectations come true. Players who are used to playing on winning teams expect to win when they move to other teams. A lot of the other topics already discussed contribute to winning. Concentration, giving good effort, practice, execution under pressure—these all play separate and definable roles in success. It is important to understand the vital connection between winning and the factors that contribute to winning.

Sure, there are times when you can win just by showing up. Every level and every league in youth baseball has probably had a "stacked up" team that made the rest of the league look as if it belonged in a different division. I have never wanted my kids to play on one of those teams. That sort of participation does not show that results are related to hard work, concentration, effort, etc. By the end of the season, those teams typically are simply going through the motions and having trouble getting excited even about picking up their first-place trophy.

The list of factors that contribute to winning is the subject of a whole lot of books—some good, some not so good. But that's not what this book is about. In no particular order, here is a list of things baseball can teach that go into a winning effort.

- Sustained effort
- Teamwork
- Self-sacrifice

- Concentration
- Talent
- Determination
- Practice
- Planning
- Courage
- Confidence
- A little bit of luck

I can preach these factors in the abstract until I am as blue in the face as a Dodger's cap, but that will never substitute for playing on a team that wins, and experiencing what it takes to do so.

In addition to learning about the effort and factors it takes to win, you must understand how to act when you do win. I want to teach what it means to be a "good winner," as that term is commonly used. A good winner compliments the efforts of those he has defeated. You do not gloat, brag, or "show up" the other team or any player you have bested.

I do not like the Golden Rule requirement for being a good winner—"be a good winner because that's how you'll want people to act when they beat you."

That's all well and good. Children understand it readily, and it does have a solid piece of New Testament backing. However, the concept is more fundamental than that. I want the boys to learn to be gracious winners, not because what goes around comes around (though it surely does), but because they should (1) have the honesty and knowledge to appreciate the efforts and talents of their adversaries and (2) be mature enough gentlemen to understand that gloating is off-limits because it is rotten behavior, not because they don't want someone to gloat at them in the future. In other words, not gloating is something you do for you, not for the other guy.

You can try to describe the precise attitude in lots of ways—class, grace, dignity—and we need to teach our children the feelings and behaviors that these words describe. Letting them win a few games on the baseball diamond to practice these skills is more important than giving them a stadium full of lectures about it. As a wise coach I know says: "You can't learn to ride a bicycle sitting on the porch."

Lesson #1
We Love You

Yep. This is perhaps the most important lesson of all. Whatever it is that you choose to do, in life, in love, or in the bottom of the sixth with two out, your mom and I will still love you. It may be that you double in two runs to win the game in the bottom of that last inning. It may be that you stand and watch a big, fat hanging curve ball for a called strike three. But your mom and I will love you just the same.

This rule will continue to apply. You may make a 34 on the ACT and have college recruiters beating down the door to award scholarships, or you may not make it out of ninth grade and land a job that barely pays rent, but we won't love you any less. Sometimes, we may be more happy or less happy with you. There will be days when we are unquestionably prouder of you, and days when our pride has gone before a little bit of destruction, but we won't love you any less.

It may be that you knew that already. You may even have known it with all your heart and been embarrassed when we told you so a time or two in front of other adults, or your cool friends. Baseball gives us a chance to both tell you and prove it to you.

We have eaten enough concession stand food to give coronary artery disease to an entire September roster. We have missed weddings, funerals, work obligations, anniversary trips, parties, sleeping late on Saturday mornings, breakfasts, lunches, and dinners to go to the ballpark. We have watched you play in searing heat, pouring rain, baking sun, drenching humidity, and wind so cold our eyes watered. We have put up with angry coaches, obnoxious teammates, rude parents, bratty siblings, pompous umpires, hungry mosquitoes, and angry wasps. And on every one of those occasions there was no place else in the world we wanted to be.

We were angry and embarrassed the afternoon you came in hard at home plate and almost knocked the other team's catcher unconscious when he didn't even have a play.

We saw you take the mound with the bases loaded and no one out in a league where more than half the kids were three years older than you were, and you got out of it in four pitches with only one run crossing the plate.

We were there the night when, for the second time in the same game, you got tagged out in the mouth while wearing braces, and your team got eliminated from the tournament while you sat in the grass outside the fence and bled.

We were there for you when you tried out for the school team and didn't make it.

I was too close when you cranked one off the tee without looking and broke my nose, and I was there two nights later when you hit an inside-the-park home run.

We saw it when as a seven-year-old, playing pitcher position in the machine pitch league, you covered first to get out an incredulous hitter on a swinging bunt.

We were there when your machine pitch team lost its first twelve in a row, and we were there the night you finally won one.

We were there for coach pitch when you had the league's orneriest coach, you hit a line shot between his legs, and he gave you the game ball for it.

We heard it the night your team questioned so many calls